Sunset

Quick & Easy
DINNERS

BY THE EDITORS OF SUNSET BOOKS
AND SUNSET MAGAZINE

LANE BOOKS · MENLO PARK, CALIFORNIA

ABOUT QUICK AND EASY DINNERS

This book is designed to help all women or men who have the responsibility for preparing dinner. Each of its seven chapters is designed to meet a different dinner preparation problem. One chapter is devoted to dinners that can be put together in an hour or less. Another chapter is filled with dinner ideas that can be made ahead when time is more plentiful, and then cooked quickly when meal-time is rushed. For the busy person who likes to entertain, one chapter contains numerous simple, yet elegant dinner party menus. Still another chapter treats the problem of cooking for only two people. Other chapters offer delicious low-calorie meals, family and company suppers, and there is even a chapter on picnics and barbecue menus.

While all these dinners make cooking quicker and easier, they do not compromise on quality. The menus in this book will help you out of "dinner ruts," for the recipes are unusual and exciting, as a quick glance through the book will show you. Don't be frightened by the exotic names of many recipes. They sound "gourmet," and they *are*; however, they are also easy to cook.

Following each menu list is a valuable introduction to the dinner. This section tells you exactly how to go about cooking the meal. It gives instructions on when to start chilling or cooking a particular dish and for how long. Also explained are what dishes to prepare first and in what order to serve them. If you've never cooked in your life, this book is especially for you because timing of meals is one of the most difficult aspects of cooking. Just follow the instructions given with each menu, and the main dish should be ready to serve at the same time as the rest of the meal—no overcooked vegetables and undercooked meat, or vice versa.

Don't feel you must serve every dish listed on any given menu. In many menus, recipes are given for the main dish and one other accompaniment or dessert, while other dishes are merely suggested. And even though recipes may be given for the entire meal, use the menus as skeletons on which to build your own meals. If you wish to cook only the entrée and serve other foods you have on hand, go right ahead. But should you need a complete dinner menu, with all the dishes tested for taste compatibility, every menu meets this standard.

Fifth Printing August 1969

CONTENTS

Serve lightly browned halibut steaks as the main dish for a quick-to-cook meal. Accompany with green salad, broccoli, bread. Menu and recipes on page 18.

Quick Family Dinners

The menus in this chapter are designed as family meals to prepare in an hour or less. They take advantage of every possible shortcut in preparation, yet offer new and delicious dinner ideas. Quick and easy cooking methods, such as broiling and sautéing are employed. "Out of the can and into the oven" is almost true of many of the meals. Others require a minimum of cooking on top of the range. The resultant dinners are often simple and economical, but provide especially good flavor combinations.

The main dishes vary from beef, veal, lamb, pork, and liver, to chicken and seafood. These recipes provide fresh approaches to old stand-by foods and help keep family dinners from settling into a dull routine. Try some or all of the dishes in each menu, and you'll find yourself building a whole new repertoire of family dinners.

Menu

Butter Lettuce
Blue Cheese Dressing
Corned Beef Bake
Frozen Chopped Broccoli
Garlic Buttered Rye Toast
Wine-Glazed Fruit   Macaroons

The corned beef casserole around which this menu is planned saves time because it needs little chopping of ingredients. If you are unable to find the twist-shaped macaroni, substitute elbow macaroni. As the casserole bakes, you can put the finishing touches on the meal.

Use prepared garlic butter or make your own, and spread it over buffet rye slices on a baking sheet. They will toast to buttery crispness as the casserole bakes. Before you serve dinner, arrange the fruits in a pan and spoon the wine and butter topping over them. The fruit can broil as you clear away the main course dishes.

Corned Beef Bake

6 ounces (about 3 cups) macaroni twists
1 can (10½ oz.) condensed cream of celery soup
½ cup milk
½ cup warm water
    Dash pepper
1 tablespoon dill seed
1 tablespoon prepared horseradish
1 jar (2 oz.) sliced pimiento, drained
1 can (12 oz.) corned beef, cubed
    Buttered bread crumbs

Cook macaroni in boiling salted water until tender, about 7 minutes. Drain, rinse with hot water, and drain again. While macaroni is cooking, com-bine soup, milk, water, pepper, dill seed, and horseradish; cover and heat to boiling, stirring occasionally. Add pimiento and corned beef. Place macaroni in buttered 1½-quart casserole; add the corned beef mixture and mix to blend. Top with crumbs. Bake, uncovered, in a moderate oven (350°) for about 20 minutes. Makes 4 servings.

Wine-Glazed Fruit

1 can (1 lb.) cling peach halves, drained
1 can (8½ oz.) sliced pineapple, drained
2 bananas, cut into quarters
3 tablespoons brown sugar
3 tablespoons soft butter or margarine
    Dash of cloves
    Dash of salt
¼ cup muscatel or red or white port

Place fruits in a foil-lined shallow baking pan. Blend brown sugar and soft butter or margarine with cloves and salt; dot over fruits. Pour muscatel or red or white port over fruits and broil, basting frequently, until lightly browned, about 8 minutes. Makes 4 generous servings.

Menu

Upside-down Hamburg Pie
Slaw with Oranges and Raisins
Cookies
Ice Cream

The main dish of this economical family dinner can be made with a minimum of time and of pan-washing. While it bakes, mix the salad. Serve any favorite ice cream and cookies for dessert.

Upside-down Hamburg Pie

1 onion, chopped
2 tablespoons shortening
1 pound ground beef
1 teaspoon salt
2 canned green chilies, chopped
¼ teaspoon oregano
1 can tomato soup, undiluted
2 cups biscuit mix, prepared according to directions on package
½ cup shredded cheese (preferably jack)

In a 10-inch frying pan, cook onion in shortening until wilted. Add ground beef, salt, green chilies, and oregano. Cook until brown, breaking meat with a fork. Add undiluted tomato soup, and heat. Pat out biscuit dough on a piece of waxed paper to a 10-inch circle, then place paper side up on top of the "filling." Peel off paper and bake in a hot oven (425°) for 20 minutes or until brown. Turn upside down on a hot chop plate; sprinkle with shredded cheese and slip under the broiler until the cheese has melted. Makes 6 generous servings.

Slaw with Oranges and Raisins

1 quart finely sliced cabbage
¼ cup seedless raisins
2 oranges, peeled, seeded, cut in small pieces, or use 1 can (11 oz.) mandarin oranges, drained
2 tablespoons finely minced onion
½ cup mayonnaise
½ cup sour cream
 Salt to taste (about 1 teaspoon)

Combine the cabbage with the raisins and oranges. Blend together the onion, mayonnaise, and sour cream; add to the salad and mix well, adding salt to taste. Makes 6 to 8 servings.

Menu

Cream of Tomato Soup
Toasted Shredded Wheat Crackers
Noodle and Spinach Casserole
Raw Vegetable Sticks
Fresh Dates and Apples
Cheddar Cheese

Here is a colorful, but simple casserole meal. The casserole makes use of leftover cooked lamb, beef, veal, chicken, ham, turkey, or pork, whichever you have on hand. It bakes in about half an hour, and the rest of the meal can be prepared while it bakes.

Use your own recipe for the tomato soup or use canned or dehydrated soup mix. You might choose celery, carrots, green pepper strips, and green onions for the raw vegetable sticks. Serve the dates and cheese with slices of unpeeled red apple.

Noodle and Spinach Casserole

8 or 9-ounce package of narrow noodles cooked and drained
2 tablespoons melted butter or margarine
   Salt to taste
   Pepper to taste
1 package (10 or 12 oz.) frozen chopped spinach, or 2 bunches fresh spinach, cooked and drained
   About 1 cup sliced mushrooms, sautéed in about 2 tablespoons butter (canned mushrooms, drained, may be used)
1½ to 2 cups diced cooked lamb, beef, veal, chicken, ham, turkey, or pork
1½ to 2 cups sour cream or gravy (canned beef gravy may be used)
   Buttered bread crumbs

Mix cooked noodles with melted butter, salt, and pepper. Mix cooked spinach with mushrooms. Combine diced cooked meat with sour cream or gravy. Season to taste. Arrange half the noodles in a greased 2-quart casserole; add the meat mixture in a layer, and then the spinach. Top with the remaining noodles and sprinkle with buttered crumbs. Before serving, put in a moderate (350°) oven for 30 minutes, or until thoroughly heated and brown. Makes 6 servings.

Menu

Veal in Paprika Cream
Noodles
Buttered Broccoli
Sliced Tomatoes
Pears
Gouda Cheese

The veal simmers until tender in a lightly seasoned Hungarian-goulash sauce while you prepare the rest of this meal. Broccoli, tomatoes, and pears round out the menu. Serve the veal on the drained noodles and season the broccoli with melted butter (lightly browned if you like). Arrange pears and a small whole Gouda cheese on a board for an attractive dessert.

Veal in Paprika Cream

1 large onion, chopped
1 small clove garlic, chopped
2 tablespoons salad oil
1 teaspoon salt
2 tablespoons paprika
1 large tomato, peeled and diced
1½ pounds veal round steak, cut in cubes (discard bone)
1 pint (2 cups) sour cream
1 package (7 or 8 oz.) egg noodles
   Minced parsley

Cook onion and garlic in salad oil until golden. Add salt and paprika, and blend well. Add tomato and veal to onion mixture. Cover and simmer gently for 45 minutes or until meat is tender. Blend in sour cream; do not boil. Serve with hot boiled egg noodles and garnish with minced parsley. Makes 6 servings.

Menu

Pan-Broiled Beef Cakes

Monterey Enchiladas

Green Salad

Mexican Chocolate

Orange Wafer Cookies

No complicated sauces or techniques are required to make these mild cheese-drenched enchiladas. Simple but appropriate additions to the menu are thick, pan-browned (or barbecued) ground beef patties and a lettuce salad mixed with an oil and vinegar dressing. The light dessert is cinnamon-flavored hot chocolate made in the Mexican fashion; serve it with orange-flavored cookies.

Assemble the enchilada casserole and while it bakes, cook the meat and mix the salad. Also gather the ingredients for the chocolate; whip the cream and chill during supper.

Fold sauce-dipped tortilla over cooked onion and green pepper mixture and cheese strips.

Monterey Enchiladas

3 tablespoons salad oil
2 large onions, thinly sliced
2 large green peppers, seeded and chopped
   Salt
2 cups (1 pt.) sour cream
2 cans (10 oz. each) enchilada sauce
1 package (12) corn tortillas
1 pound soft jack cheese, cut in thick strips
2 cups (½ lb.) shredded Cheddar cheese

Heat oil in a wide frying pan and add onions and peppers; cook until vegetables are soft. Season with salt to taste. Turn mixture into a smaller container and set aside. In the frying pan blend sour cream and enchilada sauce and heat, stirring just until simmering. Remove from heat. Dip a tortilla in sauce and let stand for a few seconds to soften. Place tortilla in a shallow baking dish, and spoon about 1/12 of the onion mixture across the center, and top it with about 1/12 of the jack cheese. Fold tortilla around filling. Repeat this procedure until all tortillas are filled, and arrange them close together in the dish. Ladle remaining sauce over casserole and sprinkle the tortillas evenly with Cheddar cheese. Bake in moderately hot oven (375°) for 20 to 25 minutes, or just until cheese inside enchiladas is melted; cut into a center enchilada to test. Serve at once. Makes 6 servings.

Mexican Chocolate

6 cups milk
¾ teaspoon cinnamon
6 ounces sweet cooking chocolate, coarsely chopped
½ cup heavy cream, whipped stiff with 2 tablespoons sugar
6 cinnamon sticks (optional)

Heat milk with ¾ teaspoon cinnamon until steaming. Add chocolate and stir until melted. With a rotary mixer, beat until mixture is frothy. Have ready the cream whipped with sugar. Pour hot chocolate into cups and top each with a spoonful of the cream. Drop a cinnamon stick in each cup if you wish. Makes 6 servings.

Menu

German Lamb with Noodles
Sour Cream Cabbage
Green Salad
Cherry Crunch

The hearty German lamb dish in this menu is complemented by the cabbage with sour cream and a crisp green salad.

Start preparation for the meal by making the lamb dish; while it cooks you can prepare the rest of the menu. Assemble the Cherry Crunch and put it in to bake; it should be served warm. Then make the sour cream cabbage and your favorite salad.

German Lamb with Noodles

  2 tablespoons flour
  1 teaspoon salt
 ¾ teaspoon dill seed
 ½ teaspoon celery seed
 ½ teaspoon caraway seed·
 ¼ teaspoon pepper
 ¼ teaspoon savory
 ¼ teaspoon rosemary
1¼ pounds lean lamb, cut in 1-inch cubes
  1 medium onion, chopped
  2 tablespoons salad oil
  1 teaspoon tarragon vinegar
 ⅔ cup boiling water
  1 package (6 oz.) egg noodles

Mix together the flour, salt, dill seed, celery seed, caraway seed, pepper, savory, and rosemary; use to coat lamb cubes. In a frying pan, brown meat and onion in hot oil. Add vinegar and water, cover tightly, and simmer gently until tender, about 45 minutes. Meanwhile, cook noodles as directed on package. Spoon lamb over the cooked, drained noodles; serve immediately. Makes 4 to 6 servings.

Sour Cream Cabbage

  1 small head cabbage
 ¾ teaspoon salt
1½ quarts boiling water
  2 tablespoons butter or margarine
  2 tablespoons instant minced onion
  1 tablespoon flour
  1 cup sour cream
 ½ teaspoon sugar
  3 tablespoons vinegar
 ¾ teaspoon salt
   Dash pepper
   Paprika

Cut cabbage into 4 wedges and cook until just tender (10 to 12 minutes) in salted boiling water. Meanwhile, melt butter in a saucepan over low heat. Add onion; blend in flour and heat until bubbly. Stir in sour cream, sugar, vinegar, salt, and pepper. Cook until thickened, stirring constantly (do not boil). Spoon sauce over cooked, drained cabbage. Sprinkle with paprika. Makes 4 servings.

Cherry Crunch

  1 cup quick-cooking rolled oats
 ½ cup regular all-purpose flour
  1 cup sugar
 ½ cup butter or margarine
  1 can (about 1 lb.) cherry pie filling
   Cream or ice cream (optional)

Combine oats, flour, and sugar; cut in butter until mixture is crumbly. Place half of mixture in the bottom of a buttered 8-inch square baking pan; spoon in the pie filling, then spread remaining crumb mixture over top. Bake in a moderate oven (350°) for 45 minutes, or until lightly browned. Serve warm; spoon into sauce dishes and top with cream or ice cream if you wish. Makes 6 servings.

Menu

Tomato Juice
Lamb Loaf
Zucchini with Sour Cream
Parsley-Buttered New Potatoes
Individual Upside-Down Cakes

This menu is suitable for the dining room or the patio. First prepare the lamb loaf; while it bakes, cook potatoes, zucchini, and make the upside-down cakes. The cakes bake in 20 minutes and may be served warm, or you can make them ahead and serve cold.

Lamb Loaf

1½ cups ground lean lamb
 2 eggs, slightly beaten
 1 teaspoon salt
 1 cup soft bread crumbs
 ¾ cup bouillon or dry red wine
 ¼ cup minced onion
 ½ teaspoon basil
    Freshly ground pepper

Combine all ingredients thoroughly and shape into an oval loaf. Place in a shallow baking pan and bake in a moderate oven (350°) for 50 minutes, basting with the juices that form in the pan. Makes 6 servings.

Zucchini with Sour Cream

Wash 2 pounds tender young zucchini and cut off stems, but do not peel. Shred on a coarse grater. Put in a saucepan with 1 cup hot water, cover and boil for 4 minutes. Drain well; mix with 1 cup sour cream, season with salt and pepper, and heat. Serve at once. Makes 6 servings.

Individual Upside-Down Cakes

Melt ¼ cup butter and mix with ½ cup brown sugar. Divide among 6 individual pie pans. Place 1 slice pineapple in each pan with a maraschino cherry in the center hole. Prepare 1 small package (9 oz.) yellow cake mix as directed on the package. Pour cake batter over the pineapple slices to within ½ inch of the top (use remaining batter for cupcakes) and bake in a moderately hot oven (375°) for 20 minutes. Cool a minute, then turn out of pans, making sure that all the syrup is poured over the pineapple. Serve warm or cold with whipped cream or vanilla ice cream if you wish. Makes 6 servings.

Menu

Little Lamb Loaves
Frozen Potato Puffs
Brussels Sprouts with Jack Cheese
Cherry Tomatoes   Celery Sticks
Quick Blueberry Crisp

This menu is basically an oven meal. It features individual meat loaves combining ground lamb and beef. Shred jack cheese over hot, cooked Brussels sprouts for a quick "sauce".

Thirty minutes is plenty of time in which to prepare this family dinner of individual lamb loaves, potato puffs, Brussels sprouts, relishes. Blueberry dessert bakes while family eats dinner.

Make the meat loaves in muffin pans and they will bake in just 15 minutes. Frozen potato puffs bake along with the meat.

Little Lamb Loaves

  1 pound ground lamb
½ pound ground beef chuck
  2 cups soft French bread crumbs
  1 can (10½ oz.) condensed onion soup
¼ teaspoon oregano
     Mint leaves

Mix ground meats, crumbs, soup, and oregano, stirring just until blended. Spoon meat mixture into 12 ungreased 2½-inch muffin cups, pressing in lightly. Bake in a hot oven (400°) about 15 minutes or until well browned. Garnish with fresh mint. Makes 6 servings of 2 loaves each.

Quick Blueberry Crisp

  2 cans (15 oz. each) blueberries, drained
     (reserve syrup for pancakes or dessert sauces)
  1 tablespoon lemon juice
⅔ cup brown sugar, firmly packed
½ cup regular all-purpose flour, unsifted
¼ teaspoon salt
¼ teaspoon nutmeg
¼ cup room temperature butter or margarine
     Cream or ice cream for topping

Place blueberries in a buttered shallow casserole (about 6½ by 9½ inches); sprinkle with lemon juice. Mix brown sugar, flour, salt, and nutmeg; cut in butter or margarine until crumbly. Cover berries with brown sugar mixture. Bake in a hot oven (400°) for 15 to 20 minutes or until bubbly. Serve warm with cream or ice cream. Makes about 6 servings.

Menu

Hawaiian Ham and Rice
Fresh Green Beans in Onion Rings
Relish Plate
Cornmeal Muffins
Ambrosia

Here is a truly last-minute menu. Make the corn-meal muffins from a mix and while they bake, put together the rest of the meal. Radishes, ripe olives, and bread and butter pickles make a good choice for the Relish Plate. Oranges, strawberries, and bananas, plus any other fresh fruits you have on hand, would combine well for the Ambrosia. To make the attractive individual vegetable servings, tuck hot-cooked green beans inside raw Bermuda onion rings. The main dish cooks in an electric frying pan.

Hawaiian Ham and Rice

2½   cups cubed, cooked ham
⅓   cup chopped green pepper
2   tablespoons butter or margarine
1   tablespoon cornstarch
¾   cup water
½   cup pineapple juice
1   tablespoon brown sugar
1½   teaspoons dry mustard
½   teaspoon ground ginger
¾   cup pineapple chunks
1½   cups steamed rice (about ½ cup uncooked rice)

In an electric frying pan set at 300°, sauté ham and green pepper in butter until ham is lightly browned. Mix together cornstarch and water; add pineapple juice, brown sugar, mustard, and ginger. Pour cornstarch mixture over ham and green pepper. Cook over medium heat (320°), stirring con-

stantly, until sauce thickens and becomes clear. Add pineapple chunks, heat through, and serve over hot rice. Makes 4 servings.

Menu

Nut-Crusted Ham Steak
Scalloped Fresh Corn
Sliced Tomatoes
Berry Patch Pudding

The accompaniments for this unusual broiled ham steak are a delicious cross-section of fresh foods. The dessert may be made ahead and served cold, or put together just before dinner and served warm. It can bake at the same time as the vegetable casserole. Both of these dishes can be kept warm beneath the ham steak if your broiler is in the oven.

Nut-Crusted Ham Steak

Generously brush a ¾-inch-thick, cooked ham steak (about 1½ pounds) with a mild-flavored honey. Broil about 5 inches below heat for 3 or 4 minutes. Turn steak, brush top side with more honey, and sprinkle with ¼ cup finely chopped salted peanuts. Broil until nut topping is lightly toasted. Carve and serve. Makes 6 servings.

Scalloped Fresh Corn

Combine 3 cups fresh corn (cut from cob) with ½ cup sliced ripe olives, ½ to ¾ cup diced Mozzarella cheese, ¾ teaspoon salt, and ¼ teaspoon pepper. Pour into a greased, shallow 1½ to 2-quart casserole. Dot with 1½ tablespoons butter. Bake, uncovered, in a moderate oven (350°) for 25 minutes or until cheese is melted and bubbling. Makes 6 servings.

Berry Patch Pudding

    4 cups cleaned whole berries of your choice —
       olallieberries, boysenberries, blackberries,
       loganberries, strawberries
    1 cup sugar (more or less to suit taste)
    ½ teaspoon cinnamon
    ¼ teaspoon nutmeg
    2 tablespoons butter or margarine
    1 cup regular all-purpose flour
    1 tablespoon sugar
    1 teaspoon baking powder
    ½ teaspoon salt
    1 egg
    ½ cup milk
    2 tablespoons salad oil

Butter a 2-quart shallow baking dish and fill with berries. Sprinkle with about 1 cup sugar, cinnamon, and nutmeg. Dot with butter. Sift flour, measure, sift again with the 1 tablespoon sugar, baking powder, and salt. Add egg, milk and salad oil; beat until smooth. Pour evenly over berries. Bake in a moderate oven (350°) for 35 minutes. Serve warm or cold. Makes 6 to 8 servings.

Menu

Pan-Fried Liver and Bacon
Corn Soufflé with Onion Sauce
Cabbage Slaw
Peach Sundaes

Short cuts to go with this quick-cooking liver entrée include frozen corn soufflés, prepared slaw dressing, and frozen peaches on vanilla ice cream. Put the soufflés in the oven to bake, then fry the bacon and make the sauce for the soufflés. Cook the liver just before serving.

Pan-Fried Liver and Bacon

Cook 1½ pounds bacon in a frying pan until crisp; remove bacon and drain on paper towels. Pour off all but about ¼ cup of the bacon drippings. Cut 1 pound thinly sliced beef liver in strips; salt and pepper and dust with flour. Quickly brown liver strips on all sides in the bacon drippings. Serve immediately topped with the cooked bacon. Makes 4 or 5 servings.

Corn Soufflé with Onion Sauce

Bake 2 frozen corn soufflés (12 oz. each) according to directions on the package. To make Onion Sauce, cook 1 medium-sized finely chopped onion in 2 tablespoons butter until soft. Add ¼ cup heavy cream, 1 teaspoon sugar, and salt to taste; bring to a rapid boil. Spoon over servings of the soufflé. Makes 4 or 5 servings.

Menu

Liver Sauté
Potato Pancakes with Apple Sauce
Broccoli with Sour Cream
Spice Cake

Cubes of liver sautéed quickly in butter, then properly seasoned, provide good eating. Natural accompaniments are thin potato pancakes with apple sauce, and broccoli with sour cream. Make the spice cake from a package mix, and serve it warm.

Liver Sauté

 2 tablespoons salad oil
 2 tablespoons butter or margarine
1½ pounds liver (beef or calf), cut in
      ½-inch cubes
 ¼ cup minced onions
 ¼ cup minced parsley

In a frying pan, heat salad oil and butter or margarine; when butter just begins to brown, add liver cubes and onions. Stir and cook quickly just until meat is lightly browned, about 5 minutes. Add parsley and toss lightly. Serve from a heated platter with potato pancakes. Makes about 5 servings.

Potato Pancakes with Apple Sauce

 4 medium-sized potatoes, peeled and shredded
 4 tablespoons flour
 1 teaspoon salt
 ½ teaspoon freshly ground pepper
 3 eggs, well beaten
      Apple sauce

Immerse potatoes in water for 5 minutes; drain thoroughly in a colander, shaking occasionally. Pour potatoes into mixing bowl and sprinkle with flour, salt, and pepper. Add eggs and mix thoroughly. Drop large spoonfuls of batter on a hot (about 400°), well-oiled griddle. Bake until brown and crisp on one side; turn and brown other side. Serve or keep warm in oven. Serve flat or rolled with applesauce. Makes 10 cakes.

Menu

Chicken Breasts in Orange Sauce
Buttered Rice
Lettuce, Avocado, Garbanzo Salad
Poppy Seed Dinner Rolls
Persian Melon Rings   Raspberries

This meal's main dish, chicken breasts and carrots in an orange-flavored sauce, is cooked in an electric frying pan from which you also serve it. While the chicken cooks, prepare the rice and salad. Slice avocados; use well drained, canned garbanzos with an oil and vinegar dressing. Slice, peel, and remove the seeds from the melon (if melon is very large, cut rings in half); sweeten the berries. Then chill melon and berries during dinner. When ready to serve, spoon berries into the center of each melon ring, adding a dollop of sour cream.

Family buffet dinner features chicken breasts, cooked with carrots and mushrooms in an orange-flavored sauce. Buttered rice, salad, poppy seed rolls complete meal. Dessert is melon with raspberries.

Chicken Breasts in Orange Sauce

½ cup regular all-purpose flour
½ teaspoon salt
½ teaspoon paprika
   Dash of pepper
   Dash of garlic powder
6 halved chicken breasts
6 tablespoons olive oil or salad oil
1 can (3 or 4 oz.) whole mushrooms
1 can (10½ oz.) condensed cream of
   mushroom soup
½ cup chicken broth
½ cup orange juice
½ cup dry white wine (optional)
¼ teaspoon nutmeg or mace
2 teaspoons brown sugar
2 cups diagonally-sliced carrots
   (about ½ inch thick)

Blend flour, salt, paprika, pepper, and garlic powder. Coat chicken with the flour mixture. Heat oil in an electric frying pan; brown chicken breasts well on both sides in the hot oil. Drain the mushrooms, reserving liquid; scatter mushrooms over chicken. Blend soup, reserved mushroom liquid, chicken broth, orange juice, wine (if used), nutmeg, and brown sugar until smooth; pour soup mixture over chicken.

Cover and cook at 225° (or simmer in a regular frying pan over low heat) about 30 minutes or until chicken is tender. About 15 minutes before chicken is done, stir in carrots; continue cooking until tender. Makes 6 servings.

Menu

Wilted Lettuce and Tomatoes
Salmon with Sour Cream Mask
Fresh Peas with Dill Butter Sauce
Crispy Hash-Browned Potatoes
Chilled Olallieberry Soup
Sweet Cream

This salmon dish, seasoned delicately with an onion-lemon mixture, bakes under a sour cream mask in less than thirty minutes. The salad is a digression from the usual bacon-and-vinegar dressed wilted salad; it "wilts" from a browned butter and sesame seed dressing. The dessert should be made ahead so it will have time to chill thoroughly.

Wilted Lettuce and Tomatoes

Break tender lettuce leaves into salad bowl to make about 4 cups. Add 3 peeled tomatoes (not chilled), cut in thin wedges. Sprinkle with salt and freshly ground pepper. Slowly heat ½ cup (¼ lb.) butter with 3 tablespoons sesame seed until butter is lightly browned. Pour hot butter over lettuce and tomatoes and quickly cover. After 2 minutes remove cover, mix and serve. Makes 6 servings.

Salmon with Sour Cream Mask

2-pound piece of filleted salmon
1 tablespoon grated onion
  Juice of ½ lemon
½ teaspoon salt
¼ teaspoon pepper
⅛ teaspoon paprika
⅛ teaspoon liquid hot-pepper seasoning
½ cup sour cream

Place salmon in greased shallow baking dish. Combine onion, lemon juice, salt, pepper, paprika, and liquid hot-pepper seasoning. Spread over salmon. Spread sour cream on top of onion seasonings to cover surface of fish. Bake in a moderate oven (350°) for 20 to 30 minutes or until fish flakes when tested with a fork. Makes 6 servings.

Fresh Peas with Dill Butter Sauce

Cook 4½ pounds fresh peas, shelled, in boiling salted water 8 minutes or just until tender; drain. Pour over a sauce made by heating 4 tablespoons finely chopped dill pickle in ⅓ cup melted butter. Season with salt and pepper. Mix lightly and serve immediately. Makes 4 servings.

Chilled Olallieberry Soup

1 cup water
  Sugar to taste (about ⅔ cup)
4 cups fresh olallieberries (or any tart berry —
  boysenberry, raspberry, loganberry)
1½ tablespoons cornstarch
2 tablespoons water
  About 1 cup cream (optional)

In a saucepan bring to a boil the 1 cup water and sugar. Add olallieberries; bring to a boil again. Cook 1 or 2 minutes, taking care that berries do not overcook and fall apart. Blend cornstarch with

2 tablespoons water. Stir into berry mixture. Stirring gently, bring to boil again. Allow to cool; chill. Serve in sherbet glasses. Pass cream to pour over top, if desired. Makes 4 servings.

❦❦❦❦❦❦❦❦❦❦❦❦❦❦❦❦❦❦❦❦❦

Menu

Fresh Spinach Salad   Mandarin Oranges

Salmon Steaks   Mustard-Dill Sauce

Tangy Green Beans

Hot French Rolls

Frozen Banana Cake

❦❦❦❦❦❦❦❦❦❦❦❦❦❦❦❦❦❦❦

This menu is meatless but elegant. Prepare the savory mustard and dill sauce as the fish is poaching. Canned green beans are enlivened by the sprightly addition of prepared French dressing and a dash of Worcestershire. Heat the rolls in foil in a slow oven, and keep the fish steaks warm on a platter in the oven if they finish poaching before you're ready for them. If you forget to remove the cake from the freezer earlier in the day, you can thaw it quickly by taking the cake from the pan, cutting it in squares, and putting the pieces on dessert plates before you begin the other preparations for the meal.

Fresh Spinach Salad

Tear washed fresh spinach into bite-sized pieces; mix in 1 can (11 oz.) mandarin orange sections, well drained, and add your favorite oil-and-vinegar French dressing.

Tangy Green Beans

Heat 2 cans (1 lb. each) green beans in the liquid in which they are packed. Drain well, and mix in ¼ cup prepared French dressing, 2 tablespoons butter or margarine, and a dash of Worcestershire; add salt and pepper to taste. Makes 4 servings.

Salmon Steaks

4 salmon steaks, about 1 inch thick
1 teaspoon salt
1 bay leaf
1 small onion, sliced
½ lemon, thinly sliced
  Hot water
  Parsley and lemon slices for garnish
  Mustard-dill sauce (recipe follows)

Place salmon in a large frying pan; sprinkle with salt, then cover with bay leaf, onion, and the lemon slices. Add water until fish is almost covered; cover pan. Bring water to a boil, then reduce heat and simmer about 10 minutes or until fish flakes easily with a fork. Remove salmon to a heated platter and serve garnished with parsley and lemon slices. Serve the mustard-dill sauce separately. Makes 4 servings.

Mustard-Dill Sauce:

3 tablespoons butter or margarine
1½ tablespoons flour
½ teaspoon salt
½ teaspoon dill weed
⅛ teaspoon pepper
2 teaspoons prepared mustard
1¼ cups milk
1 egg yolk
2 tablespoons lemon juice

Melt butter or margarine in medium-sized pan; stir in flour, salt, dill weed, pepper, and mustard. Add milk gradually, stirring constantly; cook until sauce is smooth and begins to bubble. Beat egg yolk; stir a little of the hot sauce into it, then return sauce to pan. Stir and cook about 1 minute longer. Blend in lemon juice. Makes about 1½ cups sauce.

Menu

Basque-Style Halibut Steaks
Broccoli with Quick Mornay Sauce
Green Salad
Oil and Vinegar Dressing
Hot Fruit Pastry Stars   Ice Cream

Quickly cooked halibut, browned in olive oil and garlic in the Basque manner, has a light and hearty flavor that goes well with broccoli. The fancy looking hot pastries for dessert are simply refrigerated turnovers, freshly baked.

First, sprinkle lemon juice on fish and let it stand while you heat water to cook broccoli and preheat oven for pastries. As halibut and broccoli cook, make salad and Mornay sauce and shape pastries. Bake pastries while you eat so they will be piping hot for dessert.

Basque-Style Halibut Steaks

Juice of 1 lemon
4 large halibut steaks (1½ to 2 lbs.)
  Salt and pepper
1 egg, beaten with fork until frothy
  Flour
3 or 4 tablespoons olive oil
2 whole cloves garlic
  Lemon slices
  Parsley or watercress for garnish

Squeeze lemon juice over halibut steaks and let stand a few minutes. Sprinkle steaks with salt and pepper. Dip the steaks in the beaten egg and coat on all sides. Then dust fish with flour, shaking off the excess. Heat olive oil in a wide frying pan with garlic and cook until garlic begins to brown. Place halibut in pan and cook over medium high heat until steaks are lightly browned on one side. Turn and cook until other side is browned and fish flakes easily; takes 8 to 10 minutes. Serve with lemon slices and garnish with parsley or watercress. Makes 4 servings.

Broccoli with Quick Mornay Sauce

Trim tough ends from about 2 pounds broccoli and cut in serving-sized pieces. Drop into boiling salted water (it should almost cover broccoli) and cook, uncovered, for about 10 minutes or until stems are easy to pierce. Meanwhile, heat 1 can (6 oz.) Hollandaise sauce with 2 tablespoons shredded or grated Parmesan cheese and 2 tablespoons grated American cheese. Drain broccoli, place in serving dish and top with sauce. Makes 4 servings.

Hot Fruit Pastry Stars

Open 1 package (14 oz.) refrigerated turnovers (any fruit flavor) and separate dough into 8 squares; space apart on an ungreased cooky sheet. Make a cut from each corner of each square to

You shape refrigerated ready-to-bake turnovers into stars for this fast and fancy dessert.

within ½ inch of the center. Put about 1 tablespoon of the fruit filling in the center of each square. To make each star, fold one tip from each corner of dough into the center of the pastry square and press firmly together to seal.

Bake in a hot oven (400°) for about 10 minutes or until the pastries are light golden brown. Drizzle packaged icing over pastries while still on baking sheet. Serve hot, topped with scoops of ice cream. Makes 4 servings of 2 each, or 8 servings.

Menu

Seafood Chili with Olive Rice
Parmesan Broccoli-Romaine Salad
Toasted Cornbread Triangles
Lemon Sherbet

Fresh shrimp, crab meat, Pacific oysters, and clam juice add seafood flavors to this rich chili sauce, which you serve over hot rice.

For the salad, mix cooked and chilled broccoli flowerets (leftover or cooked ahead) with romaine. Serve with a generous sprinkling of shredded Parmesan cheese and a light oil and vinegar dressing. Ahead of time, make the cornbread from a mix or your own recipe; bake it in a round pan. Cut in triangular pieces, then split, butter, and toast. While the chili simmers, you'll have time to cook the rice and prepare the salad.

Seafood Chili with Olive Rice

    1 large can (1 lb., 12 oz.) tomatoes
    ¼ cup catsup
    1 medium-sized onion, sliced
    1 clove garlic
    2 teaspoons sugar
    ½ teaspoon liquid hot-pepper seasoning
    ¼ cup (⅛ lb.) butter or margarine
    ¼ cup flour
    1 tablespoon chili powder
    ½ cup clam juice
    ½ pound crab meat
    ½ pound fresh shrimp
    1 jar (12 oz.) fresh Pacific oysters, drained
       Salt and pepper to taste
    3 cups hot cooked rice
       Ripe olives

Simmer together for 15 minutes the tomatoes, catsup, onion, garlic, sugar, and liquid hot-pepper seasoning; strain. Melt the butter, stir in the flour and chili powder to make a smooth paste. Gradually add clam juice and tomato sauce, stirring. Boil 5 minutes. Add crab meat, shrimp, and oysters. Heat thoroughly, about 10 minutes. Add salt and pepper to taste. Arrange rice in a ring on a heated platter; center with hot seafood chili. Garnish with olives heated in some of the olive liquid. Makes 6 servings.

Oriental-style dinner features green pepper steak, steamed rice, fresh mushroom salad, ginger pears, fortune cookies. Menu and recipes on pages 24 and 25.

Make-ahead Dinners

With some parts of a meal made ahead, it is usually quite simple to have dinner on the table in a short time. The menus in this chapter are all built around this make-ahead premise: Sometimes the dessert is made ahead, sometimes the main dish or salad; in other cases, practically the entire meal is made as early as a day in advance and merely reheated. The idea is, of course, to do the make-ahead work when you have more time on your hands, so that when things become hectic you can draw upon your "savings," and still serve a delicious meal to the family.

Make-ahead meals offer an extra bonus when members of the family eat at different times. Salad and dessert, for example, can chill in the refrigerator while the entrée waits in the oven, thus keeping all the foods hot or cold until each person can serve himself.

Menu

Fricassee of Veal

Artichoke Barigoule   Noodles

Stuffed Winter Pears

When you plan a busy day, here is an easy meal to serve your family. The veal and artichokes can be cooked in the morning and reheated. Cook the noodles and arrange the fresh pears in dessert dishes just before dinner.

Fricassee of Veal

2½ pounds veal stew meat, cut in 2-inch cubes
    Water
 1 carrot
 ½ teaspoon salt
18 small white boiling onions, peeled
 1 or 2 sprigs parsley
 1 bay leaf
 1 sprig fresh thyme or 1 teaspoon dried thyme
 ½ cup (¼ lb.) butter or margarine
 4 tablespoons flour
 2 egg yolks
 1 cup light cream
 1 teaspoon lemon juice
 1 cup fresh mushroom caps

Cover meat with water, bring to a boil, and skim. Add carrot, salt, onions, and herb bouquet made by tying together in a piece of cheesecloth the parsley, bay leaf, and thyme (use a long string so bouquet can easily be removed from pan). Simmer until onions are tender, about 30 minutes; remove onions and continue cooking meat 1½ hours more, or until tender. Strain stock and boil until reduced to 2 cups. Melt ¼ cup of the butter; blend in flour. Gradually stir in stock, and cook, stirring until smooth and thickened. Beat egg yolks with cream; gradually stir into sauce. Return meat and onions to sauce. Add lemon juice and mush-

rooms that have been sautéed in the remaining ¼ cup butter. Reheat and serve on a platter with noodles. Makes 6 servings.

Artichoke Barigoule

6 artichokes, trimmed
6 tablespoons olive oil
1 onion, chopped
2 cloves garlic, minced
1 carrot, chopped
1 tablespoon minced parsley
½ teaspoon rosemary
1 cup dry white wine (or 1 cup water and
    the juice of 1 lemon)

Place artichokes in saucepan with olive oil, onion, garlic, carrot, parsley, and rosemary. Cover and cook, shaking pan a few times until onion is golden. Add wine; cover and cook until artichokes are tender, about 40 minutes. Serve hot or cold with sauce in pan. Makes 6 servings.

Stuffed Winter Pears

Peel ripe winter pears carefully and remove stems. Cut a slice from the rounded end of each pear; scoop out cores with a spoon or apple corer and fill cavities with jam or preserves (black currant is good). Place each pear, stem end down, in a goblet; replace the slices on top of the rounded ends and serve with more of the same preserves.

Menu

Mixed Green Salad

Veal Steaks in Italian Sauce

Parmesan Noodles

Bouillon-Steamed Carrots

Icy Fruit Cup   Crisp Wafer Cookies

This family dinner is built around a veal entrée which is given Italian treatment. Because the veal steaks are slowly simmered in their sauce, you can choose a less expensive veal steak cut; blade steaks or arm steaks are fine.

Start the meat first, and while it cooks, you can prepare the rest of the menu. For dessert, partially thaw a package of frozen fruits or berries; serve them in chilled, stemmed sherbet glasses with cookies you have made or bought.

Veal Steaks in Italian Sauce

3 slices bacon
1 medium-sized onion, chopped
4 veal steaks
1 small can (8 oz.) tomato sauce
½ cup vermouth or apple juice
¼ teaspoon oregano
   Garlic salt
   Pepper

In a heavy frying pan or electric frying pan, cook bacon until crisp; remove from pan and drain. Sauté onions in bacon drippings until transparent; remove from pan with a slotted spoon. Brown meat quickly in remaining bacon fat. Crumble bacon over meat; add onions, tomato sauce, vermouth or apple juice, oregano, garlic salt, and pepper to taste. Cover and cook slowly for about 1 hour, or until tender. Serve on a hot platter with Parmesan Noodles. Makes 4 servings.

Parmesan Noodles

Cook about 6 ounces thin egg noodles until tender; drain. Mix immediately with 1 well beaten egg, 2 tablespoons butter, ⅓ cup grated or shredded Parmesan cheese, 3 tablespoons finely minced parsley, salt, and pepper to taste.

Bouillon-Steamed Carrots

Slice about 8 carrots thinly crosswise. Steam quickly until tender, in 1½ tablespoons melted butter, ¼ cup water, and ½ teaspoon chicken stock base; stir occasionally while steaming.

Menu

Piccata

Fluffy Rice   Spiced Peaches

Hot Rolls with Butter

Endive and Romaine Salad

Blueberry Cream Dessert

This light supper menu for four can be made without elaborate preparations. The entrée is sautéed veal (a Swiss version of Scaloppine) with a refreshing lemon flavor and a cheese topping. Frozen blueberries are combined with a cream cheese sauce for an interesting dessert.

Start your dinner preparations with the foods that are to be served cold. First make the dessert and refrigerate it so the flavors will blend and it will be thoroughly chilled. Next wash, dry, and tear the greens and make or set out your favorite dressing. Be sure to set the spiced peaches in the refrigerator early in the day so they will be well chilled. You can do all these things well ahead of serving time if you wish, so that only the hot dishes will require your last-minute attention. Start the rice cooking, then the veal, and heat the rolls during the last few minutes before dinner.

Piccata

6 to 8 thin slices of veal
2 eggs, slightly beaten
3 tablespoons lemon juice
   Dash of salt
   Dash of pepper
   Small amount of butter or margarine
6 to 8 thin slices Swiss cheese
6 to 8 lemon wedges
6 to 8 sprigs parsley

Pound veal to ⅛ to ¼-inch thickness. Mix together eggs, lemon juice, salt, and pepper. Dip meat into this mixture, turning to moisten both sides; fry in small amount of butter or margarine until meat is browned on both sides. Top each slice of meat with thin slice Swiss cheese. Cover pan and let cook about 2 minutes, or just until the cheese is melted. Serve with hot rice and wedges of lemon; garnish with sprigs of parsley. Makes 4 servings.

Blueberry Cream Dessert

1 package (10 oz.) unsweetened frozen blueberries
1 large package (8 oz.) cream cheese
3 tablespoons powdered sugar
1 tablespoon lemon juice
½ teaspoon cinnamon

Thaw the unsweetened blueberries. If frozen sweetened blueberries are used, drain the berries and discard the liquid; decrease the powdered sugar to taste. Beat together the cream cheese, powdered sugar (taste for sweetness), lemon juice, and cinnamon. Layer the berries and cheese mixture alternately into dessert glasses and chill until ready to serve. Makes 4 servings.

Menu

Dilled Lamb Stew
Steamed Rice, Noodles, or Potatoes
Crisp Green Salad
Banana Ice Cream
Sugar Cookies

This simple meal will appeal to both adults and children. Buy the banana ice cream and serve with homemade or store-bought sugar cookies. You can make the lamb stew ahead, refrigerate, and reheat with the addition of the sour cream. Serve the stew with or without a starchy food such as rice, noodles, or boiled potatoes.

Dilled Lamb Stew

2 pounds boneless cubed lamb
2 tablespoons shortening
½ teaspoon salt
½ teaspoon dill weed
1 cup water
1 cup sliced celery
1 cup sliced carrots
2 tablespoons flour
½ cup water
1 cup sour cream

Brown lamb in shortening. Sprinkle salt and dill weed over the meat and add the 1 cup water. Cover and simmer for 1 hour or until the lamb is almost tender. Then add celery and carrots. Continue cooking about 30 minutes or until the vegetables are tender. Blend flour with the ½ cup water and stir into the stew; cook, stirring, until thickened. Stir in sour cream; heat, but do not boil. Makes 6 servings.

Menu

Deviled Lamb Chops
Steamed Rice
Buttered Italian Green Beans
Relish Tray
Pound Cake with Fruit

Shoulder lamb chops are especially good for this dinner because they are unusually large and meaty; however, any cut of lamb chops can be used. Purchase one or two per person.

Prepare and chill a relish tray of fresh raw vegetables and pickled vegetables; you might use fresh radishes, cauliflower, and green onions, and pickled artichoke hearts, cucumbers, and mixed vegetables. Buy a frozen pound cake, defrost it as directed on the package. Serve chilled fruit with the cake; this could be frozen, thawed peaches or mixed fruit, canned fruit, or fresh, poached fruit such as pears. About 45 minutes before dinner, start preparations for the lamb chops, rice, and then the beans.

Deviled Lamb Chops

4 teaspoons prepared mustard
4 large lamb shoulder chops
1 tablespoon flour
1 teaspoon thyme
½ teaspoon garlic salt
 Dash pepper
2 tablespoons salad oil
1 medium-sized green pepper, sliced
1 medium-sized onion, sliced
4 thin lemon slices
1 small dried hot chili pepper, crushed, or 2 or 3 drops liquid hot-pepper seasoning
½ cup dry white wine

Spread 1 teaspoon mustard over one side of each lamb chop. Then combine the flour, thyme, garlic salt, and pepper; sprinkle over the four chops. Heat oil in a large frying pan, then place the chops, mustard side down, in the pan. Brown well on both sides. Arrange the green pepper, onion, and lemon slices, and crushed chili or liquid hot-pepper seasoning over the meat; pour the wine over all. Cover and simmer 20 to 25 minutes, or until meat and vegetables are just tender. Transfer meat and vegetables to a warm serving platter. Boil the remaining liquid until it is reduced slightly; pour over the meat. Makes 4 servings.

Menu

Green Pepper Steak   Steamed Rice
Fresh Mushroom Salad
Ginger Pears   Fortune Cookies

With the dessert and salad made ahead, and meat and vegetables sliced earlier in the day, this dinner takes only a few minutes to cook. Make the ginger pears and fresh mushroom salad any time in advance and have ready to serve. Buy the fortune cookies. If you wish, you can cook the main dish at the table in an electric frying pan. Steam the rice according to directions on the package.

Green Pepper Steak

1½ pounds flank steak
½ cup soy sauce
1 clove garlic, mashed
1 cup water
¼ cup peanut oil or salad oil
2 medium-sized green peppers, thinly sliced
1 medium-sized onion, thinly sliced
5 stalks celery, thinly sliced diagonally
1 tablespoon cornstarch
Tomato wedges for garnish

With a very sharp knife, cut flank steak in paper-thin slices diagonally, cutting with the grain of the meat. Combine soy sauce, garlic, and ½ cup of the water; marinate meat in this mixture for 15 minutes. Drain meat, reserving liquid. In an electric frying pan or large frying pan, heat peanut oil or salad oil until very hot (set temperature control at highest heat). Brown meat in the oil quickly (about 2 minutes); push meat to one side of pan and add green peppers, onion, and celery. Cook 2 minutes more or until vegetables are tender crisp. Mix the reserved liquid with cornstarch and remaining ½ cup water and stir into meat and vegetables; cook until liquid is thickened. Arrange on hot steamed rice and garnish with tomato wedges. Makes 4 servings.

Fresh Mushroom Salad

12 large fresh mushrooms (about ¾ pound), washed and dried
4 tablespoons lemon juice
4 tablespoons olive oil
2 tablespoons tarragon vinegar
2 teaspoons minced chives
2 teaspoons minced parsley
½ teaspoon tarragon
½ teaspoon chervil
½ teaspoon salt
½ teaspoon pepper
1 teaspoon sugar
1 teaspoon prepared hot mustard
Romaine lettuce

Slice mushrooms thinly through the crown and sprinkle with lemon juice; chill. Combine olive oil, tarragon vinegar, chives, parsley, tarragon, chervil, salt, pepper, sugar, and mustard; let stand 1 hour to blend flavors. Drain mushrooms and arrange them on a platter lined with romaine lettuce; pour over dressing. Makes 4 servings.

Ginger Pears

1 cup water
1 cup sugar
Dash of salt
3 pieces preserved ginger, sliced (about 2 tablespoons)
2 slices zest of lemon (pare 3-inch strips of peel from fresh lemon using potato peeler)
2 whole cloves
4 cups sliced fresh pears
Heavy cream

In a 2-quart saucepan combine water, sugar, salt, ginger, zest of lemon, and cloves. Bring to a boil, and add pears. Simmer gently, uncovered, until pears are tender, about 8 to 10 minutes. Cool or chill, and serve with a pitcher of heavy cream. Makes 4 to 6 servings.

Menu

Hearty Steak and Onions
Boiled Potatoes or Steamed Rice
Fresh Corn, Peas, or Asparagus
Mixed Green Salad
Apricot-Layered Dessert

Bite-sized pieces of round steak are simmered with plenty of sliced onions to serve with boiled potatoes or steamed rice for this simple but very satisfying meal.

Make the dessert several hours ahead so it will set. You can cook the entrée early in the day and reheat it for dinner. Potatoes or rice, the vegetable, and salad will need last-minute attention.

Hearty Steak and Onions

2 pounds round steak, cut in bite-sized pieces
2 tablespoons shortening or salad oil
3 large onions, sliced
1 teaspoon salt
½ teaspoon thyme
¼ teaspoon pepper
3½ cups hot water

Brown steak in shortening or salad oil in a large frying pan. Add onions and cook until tender. Season with salt, thyme, and pepper. Add hot water, cover, and simmer about 1 hour, or until meat is tender. Makes 4 to 6 servings.

Apricot-Layered Dessert

1 cup (½ pt.) heavy cream, whipped
½ cup chopped pecans or walnuts
⅔ cup sugar
2 tablespoons cornstarch
¼ teaspoon salt
3 egg yolks
2 cups milk
1 teaspoon vanilla
10 chocolate wafers, crushed
1 can (1 lb.) apricot halves, drained

Reserve ¼ of the whipped cream and some nuts for topping. Mix sugar, cornstarch, and salt in the top of a double boiler; stir in egg yolks, milk, and vanilla. Heat, stirring, over boiling water, until mixture thickens and coats a spoon, about 25 minutes; cool slightly. To assemble, spoon about 2 teaspoons wafer crumbs into each glass. Then, dividing the ingredients among the glasses, make 1 or 2 layers of custard, apricot halves, nuts, whipped cream, and more crumbs. Top with whipped cream and nuts. Chill until set. Makes 6 to 8 servings.

Menu

Green Salad with Tomatoes
Flank Steak Teriyaki
Browned Potatoes
Mushrooms Stuffed with Peas, Onions
Strawberries with Sour Cream Dip

Plan to marinate this flank steak several hours ahead of time. Also prepare the sour cream dip for dessert so it can chill thoroughly. The rest of the meal goes together quickly. At serving time, bring the steak to the table on a plank or carving board, surrounded by the vegetables.

Green Salad with Tomatoes

Mix greens and halved cherry tomatoes with French dressing. Garnish with slices of avocado.

Flank Steak Teriyaki

Marinate 1 large flank steak for several hours in a mixture of ¼ cup soy sauce, 2 tablespoons salad oil, 2 tablespoons honey, 1 tablespoon wine vinegar, 1 clove garlic, and 1 teaspoon minced fresh ginger root or ½ teaspoon ground ginger. Broil for 4 minutes on a side for rare, or to desired doneness. Slice thinly on the diagonal and arrange on a plank. Surround with potatoes and stuffed mushroom caps. Makes 6 servings.

Browned Potatoes

Drain 2 cans (about 1 lb. each) small new potatoes and sauté in melted butter until lightly browned. Makes 6 servings.

Mushrooms Stuffed with Peas and Onions

Wash ½ pound large mushrooms and remove stems (use for another purpose). Sauté caps in 3 tablespoons melted butter just until tender. Heat 1 package (about 10 oz.) frozen buttered peas and onions as directed on the package and spoon into caps. Makes 6 servings.

Strawberries with Sour Cream Dip

Blend together ½ pint (1 cup) sour cream, 1 teaspoon lemon peel, 1 teaspoon lemon juice, and ½ cup powdered sugar. Place in a serving bowl and chill. Wash 2 boxes strawberries with stems. Use stems as handles for dunking in dip. Makes 6 servings.

Menu

Puchero
Hot Buttered French Bread
Crisp Green Salad
Apple Pie

Puchero is a hearty soup-stew made of cubed meat, simmered with vegetables and served in bowls with its thin broth. Make the Puchero early in the day or the day before you plan to serve it. Buy or make the apple pie, using your favorite recipe, and reheat just before serving if you wish. Make the salad just before serving. Slice, butter, and heat the bread.

Puchero

```
 1  cup dried lima beans
    Water
 2  tablespoons butter or margarine
 1  pound cooked ham, cut in 1-inch cubes
1½  pounds lean pork shoulder, cubed
1½  cups hot water
 4  tablespoons lemon juice
 ½  teaspoon pepper
 6  slices broiled bacon, chopped
 4  medium-sized onions, chopped
 4  cups chopped celery
 1  medium-sized green pepper, chopped
 1  bay leaf
    Salt to taste
 1  small head cabbage, chopped
```

Put dried beans into a 1-quart bowl, cover with water and let stand several hours (they expand 2 or 3 times in volume). Melt butter in a large (3 to 4-quart size) pan; add the ham and pork cubes and brown over medium heat for 10 minutes. Add the 1½ cups hot water, lemon juice, pepper. Cover and simmer 1 hour.

Add the cooked bacon, onions, celery, green pepper, soaked undrained lima beans, and bay leaf. Add water to come about halfway to top of vegetables. Simmer for 30 minutes or until vegetables are tender. You may store or freeze the stew at this point. Add salt to taste.

About 15 minutes before serving, add the cabbage and simmer until it is tender but still holds its shape (don't overcook). Makes 6 to 8 generous servings.

Menu

Pork Scaloppine
Buttered Broccoli Spears
Mixed Green Salad
Brown-and-Serve French Rolls
Chocolate Custard Dessert

The main dish of this menu is adapted to the electric fry pan. For family suppers, it's an advantage to be able to keep the main dish warm at the table for second servings.

The make-ahead item in this menu is chocolate custard which you can make quickly in your electric blender. It only needs to chill for one to two hours, but may be made early in the day if more convenient. While the Pork Scaloppine cooks slowly for half an hour, you'll have ample time to cook and season the broccoli, mix the salad, and brown the French rolls.

Pork Scaloppine

1½ pounds pork tenderloin or butt, sliced thin
½ cup unsifted all-purpose flour
2 tablespoons butter or margarine
2 tablespoons salad oil
½ cup sherry
¼ cup water
½ cup chopped green onion
1 clove garlic, minced or mashed
1 teaspoon salt
¼ teaspoon thyme
¼ teaspoon rosemary
¼ teaspoon oregano
⅛ teaspoon pepper
2 cups fresh mushrooms, sliced

Pound meat slices as thin as possible. Dredge in flour and brown quickly in butter and salad oil in electric frying pan set at 420°. Stir in sherry and water, then the onion, garlic, salt, thyme, rosemary, oregano, and pepper. Cover and cook over low heat (225°) for 30 minutes, adding a little more water if needed. Add mushrooms, cover and cook 15 minutes more. Makes 4 to 6 servings.

Chocolate Custard Dessert

3 egg yolks
½ cup sugar
½ teaspoon vanilla
2 squares (1 oz. each) unsweetened chocolate, quartered
1 cup milk, light cream, or heavy cream
    Nuts or whipped cream for garnish

Combine in the blender container the egg yolks, sugar, vanilla, and unsweetened chocolate. (If you wish, melt the chocolate in the milk while the milk is heating.) Whirl on low speed until mixture is blended; turn off motor and scrape container sides with a rubber spatula. Heat milk, light cream, or heavy cream until hot but not boiling. Cover blender, turn motor on low speed, remove cover, pour in hot liquid, and blend about 10 seconds.

Pour into dishes; chill until set, 1 to 2 hours. To serve, garnish with nuts or whipped cream. Makes about 6 servings.

Menu

Lemon Pork Chop Bake
Apple-Glazed Carrots
Cracked Wheat Salad
Chocolate Tortini

Make the dessert for this simple meal ahead; it waits in the freezer until serving time. You can prepare the cracked wheat for the salad just before dinner, but allow it to chill at least 30 minutes after it has been cooked. The vegetable can be baked in the oven along with the pork chop casserole.

Lemon Pork Chop Bake

Brown 6 large pork chops on both sides in their own fat; lift from pan and arrange chops in a shallow baking dish. Top each with a thin slice of lemon. Pour evenly over chops ¼ cup catsup blended with ¼ cup water and 1 tablespoon brown sugar. Bake, uncovered, in a moderate oven (350°) for 45 minutes. Makes 6 servings.

Apple-Glazed Carrots

Combine 2 cups hot cooked diced carrots with 1½ tablespoons melted butter, 3 tablespoons brown sugar, and ¼ cup applesauce; heat and serve. If you prefer, season cold cooked carrots as suggested above; put in a baking dish, cover and heat in oven with pork chops for last 15 minutes as meat bakes. Makes 6 servings.

Cracked Wheat Salad

Mix together 2 cups cooked cracked wheat or bulgur with ½ cup Italian style dressing. Chill at least 30 minutes. Mix with about 1 quart bite-sized pieces iceberg lettuce. Season to taste with salt and freshly ground pepper. Makes 6 servings.

Chocolate Tortini

Crush enough chocolate-flavored wafer cookies to make ½ cup coarse crumbs. Place 2 teaspoons crumbs in each of 6 paper cupcake pan liners; top with a scoop of chocolate or chocolate ripple ice cream. Fill in around ice cream with remaining crumbs, sprinkling a few crumbs over the top. Freeze until ready to serve (seal in foil if you plan to make more than a day ahead). When you serve, top each with a small dollop marshmallow sauce and a maraschino cherry with a stem. Makes 6 servings.

Menu

Frankfurter Crown Roast
Raisin Stuffing
Vegetable Cabbage Slaw
Corn on the Cob
Open Peach Cream Pie

A delicious and economical frankfurter crown roast leads off this menu. You bake it indoors in the oven and then bring it outdoors if you wish. Make the peach pie early enough so it may chill before dinner. Also cook and chill the peas for the vegetable salad. The frankfurter roast can be prepared ahead, ready to bake about 45 minutes before serving time.

A family patio dinner stars a crown roast of frankfurters with a flavorful raisin stuffing.

Frankfurter Crown Roast

  5 cups soft bread crumbs
  1 medium-sized onion, finely chopped
  3 tablespoons butter
  1 cup sliced celery
  ½ cup raisins
  2 tablespoons minced parsley
  1 egg, beaten
  ⅓ cup water
  ¾ teaspoon salt
  ¼ teaspoon pepper
 10 dinner-size frankfurters
  3 slices bacon

Lightly toast bread crumbs in moderate oven (350°). Sauté onion in butter until soft. Mix toasted bread crumbs and sautéed onion with sliced celery, raisins, minced parsley, beaten egg, water, salt, and pepper. Slice frankfurters in half crosswise. Stand on cut ends in center of round serving platter, crown fashion. With a large needle and string, thread through middle of each half; tie ends securely so crown stands firmly. Mound stuffing in center. Bake in a moderate oven (350°) for 30 minutes; arrange bacon strips over top, return to oven and bake 15 minutes longer or until stuffing is set and lightly browned. To serve, snip string; serve with large fork and spoon. Makes 6 servings.

Vegetable Cabbage Slaw

  6 cups crisp cabbage, finely shredded
  1 green pepper, seeded and cut in fine strips
  2 fresh tomatoes, seeded and cut in wedges
  1 cup green peas, fresh or frozen, cooked and chilled
  ½ teaspoon celery seed
     Salt to taste
     Freshly ground black pepper
     Tangy French dressing

Mix together the cabbage, green pepper, tomatoes, and peas. Season with celery seed, salt, pepper, and French dressing. Makes 6 servings.

Open Peach Cream Pie

Prepare a 9-inch unbaked pastry shell, using a package mix or your own recipe. Peel and slice peaches to make 3 cups. Combine ¾ cup sugar, ¼ cup flour, ¼ teaspoon salt, and ¼ teaspoon nutmeg; add to peaches and mix lightly. Turn into pastry shell; pour 1 cup whipping cream over top. Bake in a hot oven (400°) for 35 to 45 minutes or until firm. Chill well before serving. Makes 6 servings.

Menu

Ham Mousse with Relishes
Marinated Vegetables
Bread and Butter Sandwiches
Angel Food Cake
Sliced Fresh Peaches and Ice Cream

When the weather is warm or the day has been a busy one, the idea of a cool supper waiting in the refrigerator is sheer delight to a cook. The ham mousse with horse-radish dressing may be prepared early in the day or even the day before it is to be served. To accompany the mousse, you might serve several chilled relishes, such as cherry tomatoes, radishes, carrot sticks, celery sticks, pickles, olives, or raw cauliflower. Marinate asparagus, green beans, and artichoke hearts in your favorite French dressing or a combination of 1 part lemon juice to 3 parts salad oil with salt and pepper to taste; chill before serving. The bread and butter sandwiches may be prepared and stored in a plastic bag. For dessert, serve your favorite angel food cake (or one from the bakery) with sliced, sweetened fresh peaches and a spoonful of vanilla ice cream (or whipped cream or sour cream).

Ham Mousse with Relishes

1 envelope unflavored gelatin
¼ cup cold water
1 tablespoon chicken stock base
1 cup boiling water
3 cups ground cooked ham
⅓ cup chopped green pepper
⅓ cup chopped celery
2 to 3 teaspoons prepared horse-radish (to taste)
1 tablespoon dried minced onion
1 tablespoon chopped pimiento
1 tablespoon lemon juice
1 cup sour cream
 Sour cream-horse-radish dressing (recipe follows)

Soften unflavored gelatin in the ¼ cup cold water. Then dissolve the gelatin and chicken stock base in 1 cup boiling water. Combine this liquid with ham, green pepper, celery, horse-radish, dried minced onion, chopped pimiento, lemon juice, and sour cream. Mix thoroughly and pour into a 5 to 6-cup mold. Chill until set. Serve with sour cream-horse-radish dressing and chilled vegetables. Makes 4 to 6 servings.

Sour Cream-Horse-radish Dressing:

Combine 1 cup sour cream with 1½ teaspoons prepared horse-radish and a dash of salt. Let stand several hours in the refrigerator to chill and blend in flavor.

Menu

Chicken Tarragon

Boiled New Potatoes

Asparagus with Brown Butter

Sliced Tomato Salad

French Dressing

Scones with Honey Butter

Frothy Lemon Pie

To assemble this dinner in minutes, make the pie earlier in the day. While the chicken cooks, make the scones from a packaged mix, cook the vegetables, and arrange the salad plates.

Chicken Tarragon

    1 frying chicken (about 2½ lbs.), cut up
    ¼ cup flour
    1 teaspoon salt
    ¼ teaspoon pepper
    1 clove garlic, minced or mashed
    2 tablespoons butter or margarine
    1 tablespoon bacon drippings
    2 tablespoons chopped green onion
    1 tablespoon chopped parsley
  1½ tablespoons butter or margarine
  1½ tablespoons flour
  1½ cups dry white wine
    2 tablespoons finely chopped fresh tarragon, or
       1 teaspoon dry tarragon
       Salt and pepper to taste
    1 cup (½ pint) sour cream

Dust chicken with the ¼ cup flour, salt, and pepper. Set electric frying pan at 350°; brown chicken and garlic in the 2 tablespoons butter and bacon drippings. Pour off excess fat. In a small saucepan or frying pan, sauté onion and parsley in the 1½ tablespoons butter about 2 minutes.

Stir in the 1½ tablespoons flour and allow to brown. Gradually stir in wine; bring to a boil. Add tarragon and salt and pepper to taste.

Pour sauce over chicken, cover, and cook over low heat (about 225°) for 45 minutes, or until chicken is tender; stir occasionally. Serve with sauce and a sour cream topping. Makes 4 servings.

Frothy Lemon Pie

    6 eggs, separated
    ½ cup sugar
    1 teaspoon grated lemon peel
    ⅓ cup lemon juice
    ⅛ teaspoon salt
    3 tablespoons sugar
       9-inch pastry shell, baked and cooled

Beat the egg yolks and the ½ cup sugar with an electric mixer until very thick and pale yellow. Gradually beat in the lemon peel, juice, and salt. Pour mixture into the top of a double boiler and set over simmering water. Cook, stirring constantly, until smooth and thickened, about 8 minutes. Set aside to cool slightly. Beat egg whites until soft peaks form; gradually add the 3 tablespoons sugar, beating until glossy. Fold the slightly cooled custard mixture into the beaten egg whites and spoon the mixture into the pastry shell. Bake in the top half of a moderate oven (350°) for 15 to 20 minutes or just until filling is set and lightly browned on top. Let cool before serving. Makes 6 to 8 servings.

Menu

Turkey Royale
Hot Buttered Cornbread
Green Bean Salad   Sliced Tomatoes
Orange Sherbet

The casserole in this menu provides a delicious way to use leftover turkey. You can assemble the rest of the meal quickly if you have the casserole prepared and the green beans and tomatoes chilled.

Make the casserole early in the day and refrigerate it until about one hour before serving. Use your favorite recipe for the cornbread, or use a mix, and bake it during the last fifteen minutes as the casserole bakes. Put together the salad and slice the tomatoes while the casserole is in the oven.

Turkey Royale

 2 tablespoons butter
½ pound fresh mushrooms, sliced
¼ cup (⅛ lb.) butter
 3 tablespoons flour
    Dash of cayenne
½ teaspoon dry mustard
¾ cup turkey or chicken broth
¾ cup light cream
½ cup dry white wine (or 6 tablespoons
    water and 2 tablespoons lemon juice)
 1 can (2 oz.) pimiento, drained and chopped
 1 cup shredded sharp Cheddar cheese
 5 cups sliced cooked turkey
 1 can (4½ oz.) sliced olives

Melt the 2 tablespoons of butter in a frying pan and add mushrooms; sauté for 10 minutes over medium heat; reserve. In another pan, melt ¼ cup butter and stir in the flour, cayenne, and mustard until blended. Add ¾ cup turkey or chicken broth and ¾ cup light cream, stirring until smooth. Cook stirring over low heat until thickened and smooth. Stir in white wine. Add pimiento and ½ cup of the Cheddar cheese, and stir until cheese is melted.

Butter a 2-quart casserole and arrange in bottom a layer of sliced cooked turkey, using about 2½ cups of meat. Top turkey layer with half of the sliced olives and half of the mushrooms. Pour half the sauce over the top. Cover with second half of turkey, olives, mushrooms, and remaining sauce. Sprinkle with ½ cup more Cheddar cheese, and bake, uncovered, in a moderate oven (350°) for 1 hour. If you bake cornbread in the same oven, reset oven at 425° after casserole has baked 30 minutes; bake 15 minutes more. Serve the casserole over hot buttered cornbread. Makes 6 servings.

Green Bean Salad

Chill 1 can (1 lb.) French-cut green beans. Drain and arrange over about 2 quarts crisp salad greens in bowl. Sprinkle over 6 tablespoons olive oil or salad oil and 3 tablespoons tarragon vinegar; mix. Season to taste with salt and pepper. Makes 6 servings.

Menu

Seafood Surprise
English Muffin Halves
Buttered Mixed Vegetables
Grapefruit Cream Cheese Mold
Chocolate Cake

If you make the cake and molded salad early in the day, the vegetables need be your only "kitchen cooking" for this menu. You may also wish to make the seafood sauce in the kitchen, then reheat it at the table. Plan to have your toaster on the table so you can pop in the English muffin halves to be served with the bubbling hot entrée. Make the cake from your own recipe or a mix, or buy a frozen cake.

Seafood Surprise

¼ cup butter or margarine
¼ cup flour
½ teaspoon salt
¼ teaspoon pepper
 2 cups milk
 2 teaspoons Worcestershire
 2 teaspoons marjoram
½ pound or 1 can (6½ oz.) crab meat
¼ pound or 1 can (5 oz.) shrimp
 1 small can (3 or 4 oz.) sliced mushrooms
 3 tablespoons sliced green olives
 4 English muffins, split and toasted
    Paprika

Melt butter in electric frying pan set at 250°; stir in flour, salt, and pepper. Add milk gradually, stirring until smooth. Add Worcestershire and marjoram; continue cooking until thickened. Add crab, shrimp, mushrooms and their liquor, and olives. Heat through. Serve over the toasted English muffin halves; sprinkle with paprika. Makes 4 servings.

Grapefruit Cream Cheese Mold

 2 envelopes (2 tablespoons) unflavored gelatin
½ cup cold water
 1 cup boiling water
⅓ cup sugar
¾ teaspoon salt
 3 cups fresh grapefruit pieces and juice (with all rind and membrane removed)
    Few drops red food coloring, optional
 1 large package (8 oz.) cream cheese
 2 tablespoons light cream
 1 tablespoon sugar
    Dash salt
 1 cup chopped pecans

Soften the gelatin in the cold water; add the boiling water and stir until gelatin is dissolved. Add the ⅓ cup sugar, ¾ teaspoon salt, grapefruit, and food coloring (if used). Pour half of this mixture into a 6-cup ring mold and refrigerate until set. Beat the cream cheese with the cream, 1 tablespoon sugar, and dash salt. Stir in the nuts and spread over the set layer of gelatin. Pour the remaining gelatin into the mold and refrigerate until set. Garnish with fresh berries (or pomegranate seeds when in season), if you wish. Makes 8 servings.

Menu

Cold Poached Salmon   Caper Sauce
Corn on the Cob
Tomatoes Stuffed with Potato Salad
Streusel Pear Pie

You cut through crunchy brown streusel topping and tender Bartlett pears to serve this pie.

Almost everything on this menu can be prepared in the morning, leaving you free for the rest of the day. Make up your favorite potato salad and chill it with the salmon and sauce. Just before dinner, cook the corn. Also cut medium-sized tomatoes in wedges almost to the bottom of each; then spread apart and top each one with a spoonful of potato salad. The pie may be served warm or cold.

Cold Poached Salmon

1 quart water
4 whole black peppers
1 bay leaf
2 tablespoons vinegar
2 teaspoons salt
4 salmon steaks

In a large saucepan, combine water, whole black peppers, bay leaf, vinegar, and salt; bring to simmering point. Tie salmon steaks in cheesecloth, place in water, and simmer 5 to 10 minutes, until fish flakes when tried with a fork. Drain and chill thoroughly. Makes 4 servings.

Caper Sauce:

Combine ½ cup mayonnaise, 1 teaspoon lemon juice, and 1 tablespoon chopped capers. Chill thoroughly. Makes about ½ cup sauce.

Streusel Pear Pie

½ cup granulated sugar
1 teaspoon cinnamon
2 tablespoons lemon juice
1½ tablespoons quick-cooking tapioca
6 cups peeled, cored, and sliced
   Bartlett pears
   9-inch unbaked pastry shell

Streusel Topping:

½ cup butter or margarine
½ cup firmly packed brown sugar
1 cup regular all-purpose flour

Blend granulated sugar with cinnamon, lemon juice, tapioca, and pears. Let stand 15 minutes. Pour fruit into pastry shell.

To make topping, cut butter into brown sugar and unsifted flour until mixture is crumbly (or crumble with your fingers). Pat crumbs evenly over pears. Bake in a moderately hot oven (375°) for 45 to 50 minutes, or until crust is well browned. Serve warm or cold.

Low-calorie Chicken Oriental is served here with rice, tomato juice cocktail, cucumber sticks with yogurt sauce, and sesame wafers. Menu and recipes on pages 42 and 43.

Low-calorie Dinners

Each menu in this chapter contains 600 or less calories if you eat the size servings suggested in the recipes. Most reducing diets are based on about 1200 calories per day, and a typical way to divide the calories is 300 for breakfast, 300 for lunch, and 600 for dinner.

The special benefit of these menus is that they are not only quick and easy to prepare, but are complete from appetizer to dessert and still are below the 600-calorie count. Even though you may not be on a diet, you'll find such menus come in handy after lazy vacations or festive holidays when you'd like to cut back on rich foods for a time. Nor will you be reluctant to serve these dinners to guests, for each meal is delicious, filling, and high in food value; if your guests happen to be counting calories, too, they'll appreciate the dinners even more.

Menu

Green Consommé
Burgundy Beef
Hot Spinach Salad
Melon Compote

If you are expecting guests who are interested in cutting calories, here is a meal that qualifies. Prepare the melon compote and chill. You can also start the meat ahead and let it marinate in the refrigerator. Hard cook an egg for the salad. Everything else can be prepared quickly just before serving.

Green Consommé

Force through a wire strainer (or whirl in a blender) 1 cup frozen peas and 1 can (14 oz.) chicken broth. Heat to simmering; flavor with 1/16 teaspoon curry powder and serve. Makes 4 servings.

Burgundy Beef

1 pound sirloin steak, fat trimmed, sliced across the grain in ⅛-inch slices
¼ pound fresh mushrooms, thinly sliced
½ cup dry red wine
1½ tablespoons butter or margarine
¼ teaspoon crumbled chervil
¼ teaspoon tarragon
¼ teaspoon salt
⅛ teaspoon marjoram
1½ tablespoons flour

Combine steak slices with mushroom slices; place in a small bowl and cover with wine. Let stand at least 15 minutes at room temperature, or for 1 hour or longer in the refrigerator. Drain meat and mushrooms thoroughly, saving liquid. In a frying pan, melt butter or margarine with chervil, tarragon, salt, and marjoram. Add meat; stir and cook over medium heat until meat loses pink color. Sprinkle with flour, and blend in wine marinade. Cook until slightly thickened. Makes 4 servings.

Hot Spinach Salad

1 hard-cooked egg, finely chopped
2 teaspoons minced parsley
1 small green onion (white part only), chopped
¼ teaspoon dry mustard
¼ teaspoon salt
¼ teaspoon pepper
1 tablespoon salad oil
3 tablespoons red wine vinegar
1½ pounds hot cooked spinach

Combine hard-cooked egg, parsley, green onion, dry mustard, salt, pepper, salad oil, and red wine vinegar. Pour over the spinach. Makes 4 servings.

Melon Compote

Chill 4 cups cut up melon (a combination of cantaloupe, casaba, honeydew, or other favorite melons, or just one kind) with grated peel and juice of 1 lime and 1½ tablespoons mild-flavored honey. Makes 4 servings.

Menu

Tangerine Juice Cocktail
Ground Beef Steaks   Onion Gravy
Broiled Tomatoes, Parmesan
Cucumber Salad
Round Sesame Seed Crackers
Pineapple with Honey Sauce
Coffee or Iced Tea

This colorful meal can be prepared in a short time since the recipes are simple. First make and chill the cucumber salad. Cut the fresh pineapple in chunks and refrigerate; also prepare and chill the honey sauce. For the tangerine cocktail, prepare 1 can (6 oz.) frozen concentrated tangerine juice as directed; serve in 4-ounce portions. Make gravy from a prepared mix. Broil the tomatoes alongside the meat. Assemble the dessert just before serving. Allow two of the sesame crackers per serving to stay within the 600 calorie limit.

Ground Beef Steaks

1½ pounds lean ground beef
 1 tablespoon lemon juice
1½ teaspoons salt
 ½ teaspoon pepper
    Onion gravy (recipe follows)

Combine the beef with lemon juice, salt, and pepper; mix well. Shape into 6 oblong steaks about ¾ inch thick. Broil 4 to 5 minutes per side about 6 inches from the broiler (cook longer if you prefer them well done). Serve topped with Onion Gravy. Makes 6 servings.

Onion Gravy:

Prepare 1 package (1 oz.) onion gravy mix as directed on the package, substituting ¼ cup red wine for ¼ cup of the water. (Or use 1 package brown gravy mix as directed above, but add 2 teaspoons instant minced onion.)

Broiled Tomatoes, Parmesan

6 medium-sized tomatoes
   Salt and pepper
1 tablespoon grated Parmesan cheese
1 tablespoon butter

Halve tomatoes crosswise; sprinkle with salt and pepper. Then sprinkle about ¼ teaspoon Parmesan over each tomato half; dot each with ¼ teaspoon butter. Broil for 4 to 5 minutes about 6 inches from broiler. Makes 6 servings of 2 halves each.

Cucumber Salad

 3 medium-sized cucumbers
 ½ teaspoon salt
1½ cups low fat cottage cheese
 3 tablespoons vinegar
 1 tablespoon minced parsley
 1 tablespoon green onion top
 ⅛ teaspoon pepper
    Lettuce
    Parsley

Peel, halve lengthwise, and slice cucumbers. Place in a bowl and sprinkle with salt; set aside. In the container of an electric blender (or in the small bowl of an electric mixer), combine the cottage cheese, vinegar, parsley, green onion, and pepper. Whirl (or mix) until well blended. Mix with cucumbers; chill. Serve on lettuce leaves and garnish with parsley. Makes 6 servings.

Pineapple with Honey Sauce

Peel and cut into bite-sized chunks 1 medium-sized fresh pineapple. Refrigerate chunks in a covered bowl. Meanwhile, stir 2 teaspoons honey into 1 cup yogurt. When ready to serve, arrange chunks in 6 sherbet dishes, top with the sauce and garnish with a mint leaf. Makes 6 servings.

Menu

Spinach Soup

Carrot Sticks   Bread Sticks

Roast Leg of Veal

Green Beans Steamed with Mushrooms

Sauerkraut and Apple Salad

French Bread

Almond Peach Custard

Veal is an excellent meat to choose for a low calorie menu, since it is the leanest of the popular foursome: beef, veal, pork, and lamb. In this meal for six, the diet-conscious guests can take carrots instead of bread sticks with the soup, and skip the pan juices on their portions of roast leg of veal. Even with a thin slice of unbuttered French bread, the entire dinner totals less than 600 calories.

Spinach Soup

3 cups chicken broth (freshly made, canned, or made from chicken stock base)
1 or 2 teaspoons tarragon
2 tablespoons minced onion
1 tablespoon vinegar
½ pound fresh spinach, finely chopped
    Salt to taste
1 hard-cooked egg, sliced (optional)

Bring to a boil the chicken broth and season with tarragon, onion, and vinegar. Add spinach and return to a boil. Simmer slowly 3 or 4 minutes. Season to taste with salt. (You can make this soup ahead and reheat to serve.) Serve hot; add a slice of hard-cooked egg to each bowl of soup if you like. Makes 6 servings.

Roast Leg of Veal

Allow about ¼ pound boned veal or ⅓ pound veal with bone for each serving, but for roasting, have your meatman cut a leg roast weighing at least 3 pounds. Let roast stand at room temperature for several hours. Lay several thin slices of bacon over the top side of the meat (3 slices are enough for a 3 to 6-pound roast) and sprinkle with salt. Cook in a moderately slow oven (325°) until internal temperature registers 170°, or allow about 38 minutes a pound for a 3-pound roast, 33 minutes a pound for a 6-pound roast, and 30 minutes a pound for an 8-pound roast. For additional flavor, you can insert a few slivers of garlic into meat before cooking. Allow about 15 minutes rest period before carving. Dieters should skip pan juices with bacon drippings on sliced meat.

Green Beans Steamed with Mushrooms

    1   tablespoon butter or margarine
    ¾   pound mushrooms, sliced
    1   teaspoon salt
    1½ pounds green beans, cut, or 2 packages
        (10 oz. each) frozen cut green beans, thawed

Melt butter or margarine in a shallow, heavy pan. Stir in mushrooms and salt; cover and simmer slowly for about 8 minutes, or until there is a quantity of mushroom liquid in pan. Add green beans; cover and cook until beans are done to suit your taste, stirring occasionally. Serve with juices. Makes 6 servings.

Sauerkraut and Apple Salad

    1   can (about 1 lb.) sauerkraut, drained,
        chopped coarsely
    1   tablespoon minced parsley
    ½   teaspoon caraway seed
    ⅛   teaspoon anise seed
    1   teaspoon sugar
    2   tablespoons sour cream
    1   medium-sized, unpeeled red apple, diced
        Lettuce cups

Toss sauerkraut with parsley, caraway seed, anise seed, sugar, and sour cream. Cover and chill several hours. Just before serving, add diced red apple. Serve in lettuce cups. Makes 5 or 6 servings.

Almond Peach Custard

    1   can (1 lb.) water-packed peach halves,
        drained
    1½ cups skim milk, scalded
    2   eggs, beaten
    3   tablespoons sugar
    ½   teaspoon almond extract
    ⅛   teaspoon salt

Place an equal portion of peaches in each of 6 individual ramekins. Blend together scalded skim milk, beaten eggs, sugar, almond extract, and salt. Pour an equal amount into each of the ramekins. Place in a pan of water, half the depth of the custards, and bake in a moderate oven (350°) for 25 minutes, or until custard is set (shake gently to test). Chill. Makes 6 servings.

Menu

Tomato Juice Cocktail

Baked Chicken Paprika

Carrot and Rice Casserole

Lemon-Dressed Green Salad

Seasoned Rye Crackers

Persian Melon with Lime Sherbet

Coffee or Nonfat Milk

This family meal is complete from appetizer to dessert, but still below a calorie count of 600 per person. A chilled tomato juice cocktail precedes baked chicken and a vegetable casserole which bake together in the oven. The green salad has a lemon dressing containing no oil. Melon with sherbet completes the meal. If you have coffee rather than milk, you save 87 calories.

Nearly an hour before dinner, prepare the chicken and the casserole; start them to bake.

Meanwhile, make the tomato juice cocktail and refrigerate. Tear salad greens and be ready to dress the salad just before serving. Have the melon chilling, and assemble the dessert after the main course is finished.

Tomato Juice Cocktail

Season 1 small can (1 pt., 2 oz.) tomato juice with 1 tablespoon lemon juice, ⅛ teaspoon salt, ⅛ teaspoon pepper, and ⅛ teaspoon Worcestershire. Chill; serve in 4 small glasses.

Baked Chicken Paprika

1   broiler-fryer, cut in pieces (omit back, liver, and giblets)
1   teaspoon paprika
¾   teaspoon salt
½   teaspoon sugar
⅛   teaspoon pepper

Wash and drain chicken pieces; arrange in a single layer, skin side up, in a buttered baking pan. Sprinkle with a mixture of paprika, salt, sugar, and pepper. Bake in a hot oven (400°) for 35 minutes; turn pieces and cook 10 to 15 minutes longer. Makes 4 servings of 2 pieces each.

Carrot and Rice Casserole

½   cup uncooked rice
1½   cups thinly sliced carrots
¼   teaspoon ground ginger
½   teaspoon grated orange peel
1   tablespoon chopped parsley
1   tablespoon instant minced onion
4   teaspoons chicken stock base, or
     2 chicken bouillon cubes
1½   cups boiling water
1   tablespoon butter

Place the rice in a shallow pan and lightly brown in a hot oven (400°) for 8 to 10 minutes. Place browned rice in a shallow, lightly buttered casserole; mix in the carrots, ginger, orange peel, parsley, and onion. Dissolve the chicken stock base or bouillon cubes in the boiling water; add butter. When butter is melted, pour chicken stock over the rice; cover and bake for about 25 minutes. Makes 4 servings.

Lemon-Dressed Green Salad

Wash, drain, and separate leaves from 1 small head romaine lettuce; arrange in a salad bowl, cover, and refrigerate. Just before serving, sprinkle with 1 teaspoon sugar, ¼ teaspoon salt, and a mixture of 1 tablespoon lemon juice and 1 tablespoon water. Toss and serve. Garnish with 4 thin slices lemon. Makes 4 servings.

Persian Melon with Lime Sherbet

Top each of 4 wedges of chilled Persian melon with a small scoop (about ⅓ cup) of lime sherbet. Sprinkle flaked coconut or toasted flaked coconut over sherbet. Makes 4 servings.

Menu

Hot Tomato Juice Cocktail
Cucumber Sticks with Yogurt Sauce
Chicken Oriental
Chow Mein Noodles or Hot Rice
Sesame Crackers
Ginger Ice

The dessert for this menu is prepared a day ahead, with extra for future meals. The salad and the ingredients for the entrée may be done early and refrigerated. Before serving, you'll need to steam the rice, heat the tomato juice, and start the entrée in a large frying pan.

Hot Tomato Juice Cocktail

3 cups tomato juice
3 whole cloves
1 tablespoon lemon juice
1½ teaspoons sugar
1½ teaspoons salt
  Dash black pepper
¾ cup dry white wine (optional)

Combine tomato juice, cloves, lemon juice, sugar, salt, pepper, and wine, if desired. Just before serving, heat (do not boil). Makes 6 servings.

Cucumber Sticks with Yogurt Sauce

1 teaspoon dill weed
½ teaspoon celery salt
½ teaspoon sugar
½ teaspoon dry parsley flakes
1 cup yogurt
1 large cucumber, peeled and sliced into 16 sticks
  Parsley for garnish

Mix dill weed, celery salt, sugar, and dry parsley flakes with yogurt. Stand the cucumber sticks up around the edge of a small bowl; pour the yogurt into the bowl and garnish with parsley. Refrigerate several hours. Makes 6 servings.

Chicken Oriental

3 whole chicken breasts
¼ cup salad oil
2 cups diagonally sliced celery
1 green pepper, sliced
5 green onions, sliced
1 package (10 oz.) Chinese (edible pod) peas, thawed
1 cup sliced bamboo shoots
¼ pound fresh mushrooms, sliced
1 can (4 or 5 oz.) water chestnuts, drained and sliced
2 cups chicken broth
2 tablespoons soy sauce
1 teaspoon monosodium glutamate
1 teaspoon sugar
1 tablespoon salt
  Dash of pepper
2 tablespoons cornstarch
¼ cup water

Remove bones from chicken breasts; slice meat in short, narrow strips. (Because the chicken and vegetables cook quickly, it is best to prepare them before you start cooking.) Sauté the chicken in salad oil until meat is lightly browned.

Add to the pan the sliced celery, green pepper, green onions, Chinese peas, bamboo shoots, fresh mushrooms, and water chestnuts. Stir and fry a few minutes until vegetables are wilted. Mix together chicken broth, soy sauce, monosodium glutamate, sugar, salt, and pepper. Pour this mixture over the chicken and vegetables; cover and steam about 5 minutes. Dissolve cornstarch in water; add to the broth and stir until liquid is thickened. Serve immediately over hot rice or crisp chow mein noodles. Makes 6 servings.

Ginger Ice

  1 package (3 oz.) lemon-flavored gelatin
  1 cup boiling water
 ½ cup sugar
 ¼ cup orange juice
 ¼ cup lemon juice
 ¼ cup pineapple juice
  2 cans (12 oz. each) low-calorie ginger ale
  3 egg whites
  2 tablespoons sugar
     Mint sprigs for garnish

Dissolve gelatin in boiling water. Stir in the ½ cup sugar until dissolved. Add orange juice, lemon juice, and pineapple juice. Pour in ginger ale. Freeze mixture until almost firm (several hours). Remove mixture from freezer, beat until mushy, and refreeze. When the ginger ale mixture is frozen again, beat 3 egg whites until stiff, gradually adding 2 tablespoons sugar. Break the frozen mixture into chunks and beat into the egg whites. Freeze this entire mixture. Before dinner, spoon the ice into serving dishes and keep in the freezer until serving time. Garnish with sprigs of mint. Makes 12 to 15 servings.

Menu

Clear Soup with Chives
Radishes   Crisp Crackers
Sherried Scallops with Almonds
Lemon Broccoli
Fresh Tomato Risotto
Mandarin Soufflé
Grape Clusters   Thin Cookies

This guest dinner is designed to please dieters and nondieters alike. Including a few grapes and one thin cooky with the fruit soufflé, the meal is well within the 600-calorie limit.

The entrée, sherried scallops with almonds, doesn't have the sound or flavor of a typical diet dish, and appears even less so when prepared at the table in a chafing dish or an electric frying pan. Start the entrée as soon as you serve the soup.

Clear Soup with Chives

Serve hot cups of well-seasoned, fresh (fat-free) or canned beef broth with finely snipped chives sprinkled over each serving. Accompany with radishes, crisped in ice water, or crackers.

Sherried Scallops with Almonds

  3 tablespoons sliced, unblanched almonds
1½ teaspoons butter or margarine
  2 tablespoons chicken broth (fresh, canned, or made from chicken stock base)
 ¼ teaspoon salt
1½ pounds scallops, cut in halves or quarters
  2 tablespoons sherry

In a chafing dish over full flame (or electric frying pan set at about 325°), lightly brown almonds in butter or margarine; set almonds aside.

*Scallops simmer in chafing dish as guests enjoy soup.
Broccoli, risotto stay hot on warming tray.*

Lemon Broccoli

Allow ⅓ pound broccoli spears for each serving. Add several thin strips of pared fresh lemon peel to cooking water and cook until broccoli is just done. Garnish with julienne strips of lemon peel. Nonweight-watchers can dot their servings with butter, but the additional richness is extraneous in this recipe.

Mandarin Soufflé

1 envelope unflavored gelatin
1 cup freshly squeezed orange juice
1 cup orange sections, or drained, canned mandarin orange sections
½ teaspoon grated orange peel
Dash of salt
3 egg whites
¼ cup sugar
Chocolate curls for garnish

Soften gelatin in orange juice and dissolve over hot water. Add orange sections (reserve a few orange sections for garnish, if desired), grated orange peel, and salt. Whip egg whites until stiff, and beat in sugar, 1 tablespoon at a time, until whites hold soft peaks. Fold in gelatin mixture. Spoon into stemmed glass serving dishes. Chill until set. Garnish with additional orange sections or a few chocolate curls (peel part of a chocolate bar with a vegetable peeler). Makes 4 or 5 servings.

Add to pan chicken broth and salt; bring to a boil. Add scallops; cover and simmer about 8 minutes or until scallops lose transparency, stirring occasionally. Return almonds to pan along with sherry and simmer for 2 minutes more. Makes 4 servings.

Fresh Tomato Risotto

2 small tomatoes, peeled and diced
¾ cup long grain rice
2 green onions, thinly sliced, including tops
½ teaspoon sweet basil
½ teaspoon salt
1¾ cups chicken broth (freshly made, canned, or made from chicken stock base)

Combine tomatoes in a 1 or 1½-quart casserole with rice, onions, sweet basil, and salt. Heat chicken broth to boiling and pour over rice. Cover and bake in a moderately hot oven (375°) for about 35 minutes or until rice is cooked; stir occasionally. Makes 4 or 5 servings.

Menu

Tomato Juice   Wheat Crackers
Crab Foo Yung
Chinese (edible pod) Peas
Pears Flambé

Even with sauce, Crab Foo Yung has only 190 calories in a serving of two patties. Fresh bean sprouts give it tender crispness. You can cut calories even more by cooking the cakes in a frying pan with a nonstick fluorocarbon finish, and omitting the oil.

Everything in this menu can be prepared quickly just before dinner. Cook the peas in small amounts of butter and water. Serve the pear dessert with cream or ice cream to diners who aren't concerned about calories. You may wish to cook the dessert at the table in a chafing dish.

Crab Foo Yung

    4 eggs, well beaten
    1 package (7½ oz.) fresh bean sprouts,
       washed and drained
  ⅓ cup (about 6) thinly sliced green onions
    1 cup (about 8 oz.) flaked, cooked crabmeat
  ½ teaspoon salt
  ⅛ teaspoon pepper
  ⅛ teaspoon garlic powder
    2 tablespoons salad oil
       Foo Yung Sauce (recipe follows)

Combine eggs, bean sprouts, onions, crabmeat, salt, pepper, and garlic powder, mixing lightly. Omit the salt if using canned crabmeat. Heat the oil in a large frying pan, using just enough to coat pan; add remaining oil as needed. Using about ¼ cup of the mixture for each, fry egg-crabmeat patties as you would pancakes, turning once. Cook until set and lightly browned. Remove to a hot platter and serve with Foo Yung Sauce. Makes 5 servings, 2 cakes each.

Foo Yung Sauce:

In a pan combine 1 teaspoon cornstarch, 1 teaspoon sugar, 2 teaspoons soy sauce, and 1 teaspoon vinegar; stir in ½ cup chicken stock or vegetable bouillon (made from a bouillon cube). Cook over low heat until thickened.

Pears Flambé

    4 tablespoons butter
    3 whole firm Anjou or Bosc pears, peeled,
       cored, and sliced
       Lemon juice or powdered ascorbic acid
       compound (optional)
    3 to 4 tablespoons sugar (or to taste)
  ¼ cup rum, brandy, or Cointreau,
       slightly heated
       Ice cream or heavy cream

Melt butter in a frying pan over medium to high heat and add pear slices. (If you peel the pears ahead, sprinkle with the lemon juice or powdered ascorbic acid compound to keep them from turning brown.) Sprinkle with sugar and heat, shaking the pan and stirring gently until pear slices are well coated with butter. Pour over them the rum, brandy, or Cointreau and ignite. Serve immediately. The pears should not be overcooked. Serve them over ice cream or with heavy cream poured over the fruit if you wish. Makes 4 servings.

Rack of lamb makes two servings of four chops each. Also on the menu; mushroom-onion skewers, peas in patty shells, wheat pilaf. Menu and recipes on pages 52 and 53.

Dinners for Two

Quick meals for two people require a special type of planning to keep food interesting with a minimum of leftovers and pan-washing. Couples, however, have the advantage of being free to serve and eat their meals all over the house in a relaxed fashion that, in a larger family, would be possible only on the children's night out. Two people can eat sitting on cushions in front of the fire, from baskets on the patio, off portable trays—almost anywhere they please.

In addition to everyday menus for two, this chapter includes several quite elegant dinners designed specifically to serve two people. Some of the old favorites, usually cooked in large quantities, have now been tested for preparing two to three servings. These more classic dinners, as well as the simpler dinners for two, are all surprisingly quick and easy.

Menu

Southern-Style Creamed Chicken

Duchess Potatoes

Green Beans with Almonds

Lettuce Wedges   French Dressing

Orange Butter Pound Cake

Creamed chicken with ham served in a broiled ring of dehydrated mashed potatoes makes a very attractive main course for two. Frozen green beans, prepared salad dressing, a simple frozen orange concentrate sauce, and frozen cake reduce the time it takes to prepare this meal. Early in the day, if convenient, set out the package of creamed chicken to thaw.

Southern-Style Creamed Chicken

1 package (14 oz. or 11½ oz.) frozen creamed chicken
¾ cup boiled ham, diced
1 tablespoon butter or margarine
½ teaspoon prepared mustard
   Duchess potatoes (recipe follows)
   Several strips sliced Cheddar or processed American cheese

Heat the thawed creamed chicken slowly to simmering in a saucepan. (Or thaw and heat according to package directions.) Cook diced ham quickly until lightly browned in butter or margarine; add to creamed chicken along with mustard. Spoon chicken into prepared ring of Duchess potatoes (recipe follows). Lay strips of cheese across the chicken. Place under broiler until cheese is bubbling and potatoes are lightly browned. Makes 2 or 3 servings.

Duchess Potatoes

Prepare a 4-serving portion of dehydrated mashed potatoes according to directions on the carton. Season with salt and 1 tablespoon butter or margarine. Beat in 2 egg yolks. On a board or oven-proof tray, spoon potatoes in a ring and brush with slightly beaten egg white. Fill as directed above.

Green Beans with Almonds

Cook 1 package (about 9 oz.) frozen green beans seasoned with almonds (see directions on the box).

Orange Butter Pound Cake

6 tablespoons thawed frozen orange juice concentrate
2 tablespoons sugar
6 tablespoons butter or margarine
   Slices of warm pound cake (bakery or frozen, thawed)

Make orange sauce by boiling together until syrupy the frozen orange juice concentrate, sugar, and butter or margarine (takes about 4 minutes). Drizzle sauce over pound cake just before serving. Makes about ⅓ cup sauce.

Menu

Fresh Pea Soup
Spinach and Tomato Salad
Chicken Breast with Mushrooms
Buttered Brown Rice
Dinner Rolls and Butter
Currant Apples with Sour Cream

This menu is designed for a special occasion for two. It is not difficult or time-consuming, but the chafing dish entrée gives it an elegant air. (If you prefer, cook the chicken in an electric frying pan, and serve it on a heated platter.)

You can make the fresh pea soup and currant apples in advance; reheat the soup before serving and refrigerate the apples until ready to serve. If you use a chafing dish, start cooking the chicken breasts about 30 minutes before you sit down at the table. Serve the soup a few minutes before the chicken is ready, and keep the rice warm during soup course. Serve warm dinner rolls.

Fresh Pea Soup

Cook 1 cup fresh or frozen peas in ½ cup water with ½ teaspoon salt. When tender, add 1 cube chicken bouillon, ¼ of a canned California green chili; ½ cup undiluted evaporated milk. Reheat; garnish with croutons. Makes 2 servings.

Spinach and Tomato Salad

Tear 1 small bunch of spinach in small pieces. Halve about 10 cherry tomatoes; mix with the spinach. Dress with French dressing just before serving. Makes 2 servings.

Chicken Breast with Mushrooms

1 whole chicken breast, cut in 2 pieces
¼ cup flour
½ teaspoon salt
⅛ teaspoon paprika
⅛ teaspoon nutmeg
⅛ teaspoon pepper
2 tablespoons butter
¾ cup heavy cream
3 tablespoons sherry
8 medium-sized fresh mushrooms, sliced

Dust chicken breasts with a mixture of the flour, salt, paprika, nutmeg, and pepper. Melt butter in a chafing dish over direct heat; brown chicken on both sides (about 15 minutes). Remove chicken, stir in ½ cup of the cream and the sherry. Return chicken to chafing dish, cover and cook slowly for about 20 minutes or until the chicken is tender. Add remaining ¼ cup cream and mushrooms; cook 10 minutes more. Serve from chafing dish onto dinner plates. Makes 2 servings.

Buttered Brown Rice

Use 1 cup quick-cooking brown rice; cook as directed on package. Stir in 2 tablespoons butter and 1 teaspoon chopped chives just before you remove it from the heat. Makes 2 servings.

Currant Apples with Sour Cream

2 cooking apples, peeled and sliced
1 tablespoon water
3 tablespoons brown sugar
¼ teaspoon grated lemon peel
¼ teaspoon cinnamon
2 tablespoons currant jelly
⅛ teaspoon vanilla
4 tablespoons sour cream
  Brown sugar

Put apple slices into a saucepan. Over the top, sprinkle water, brown sugar, grated lemon peel, and cinnamon. Cover and simmer for 10 minutes. Add currant jelly and simmer 5 minutes more or until apples are tender; stir in vanilla. Cool and chill. When ready to serve, put 1 tablespoon sour cream in the bottom of each sherbet glass, add the apple mixture, and top each with another tablespoon sour cream. Garnish with a sprinkling of brown sugar. Makes 2 servings.

Menu

Turkey or Chicken Florentine
Quick Potatoes Anna
Tossed Green Salad
Apple Dumplings or Apple Pie
Hot Pineapple Sauce

Classic dishes such as the two in this menu are especially easy to simulate when you begin with frozen poultry in a sauce and frozen pre-browned potatoes. Bake the dessert earlier in the day if you have just one oven.

Turkey or Chicken Florentine

Cook 1 package (10 oz.) frozen chopped spinach as directed on the box, but just until thawed. Drain, squeezing out excess liquid. Season with salt and spread spinach evenly in a small shallow casserole (about 1-quart size). Spoon over spinach this mixture: Heat 1 package (10 oz.) frozen turkey breast slices in sauce or 1 package (14 oz., or 11½ oz.) creamed chicken as directed on the box. Stir in ½ cup julienne strips of ham and 1 can (3 or 4 oz.) drained sliced mushrooms. Check taste for salt and pepper. Sprinkle ¼ cup shredded Parmesan cheese over the creamed layer and bake in a hot oven (425°) for 10 minutes or until bubbling. Makes 2 servings.

Quick Potatoes Anna

Empty 1 package (14 oz.) frozen browned potato slices in a single layer on a rimmed baking sheet. Heat in a hot oven (425°) for 20 to 25 minutes. Melt 3 tablespoons butter in a saucepan. Stir in 3 tablespoons minced parsley. Place potatoes in a small, deep serving bowl and pour parsley butter over them. Makes 2 or 3 servings.

Apple Dumplings or Apple Pie

Bake frozen apple dumplings or a small apple pie according to directions on the carton. Serve warm or cool with this sauce:

Hot Pineapple Sauce:

Rapidly cook 2 tablespoons butter, 4 tablespoons dark brown sugar, and the syrup drained from 1 can (about 9 oz.) crushed pineapple. When sauce is thick and beginning to caramelize, stir in the pineapple and simmer a few minutes more. Serve hot or reheat. Makes about ¾ cup sauce.

Menu

Green Salad with Tomato Wedges
Sesame Seed French Rolls (optional)
Burgundy Burgers
Hot Bananas in the Skin
Sautéed Chinese Peas
Strawberries de Luxe

Miniature barbecue was set inside fireplace for cooking patties, moved to hearth for serving.

This menu stars hamburgers, glorified with red wine and Roquefort cheese, cooked on a barbecue grill. The bananas and sautéed (edible pod) peas cook with the meat patties in less than 10 minutes.

Ahead of time, prepare the meat patties so they can marinate about 2 hours. The dessert should chill about 1 hour. Allow thirty minutes to heat up most charcoal burning grills. During this time you can prepare the salad. If you wish to include bread, wrap sesame seed French rolls in foil and place over the coolest part of the grill while the meat barbecues.

Roquefort or blue cheese on each meat patty just before serving so it will melt slightly. Makes 2 servings.

Burgundy Burgers

¾ pound ground beef chuck
2 tablespoons chopped parsley
2 tablespoons chopped green onion
¾ teaspoon salt
    Freshly ground pepper to taste
⅓ cup dry red wine
2 squares Roquefort or blue cheese

Mix together the ground chuck with parsley and green onion; season with salt and pepper. Shape in 2 patties, making a depression in the center of each one. Place in a shallow pan and pour wine over patties, pouring into the depressions. Chill 2 hours or longer. Remove meat patties from marinade and broil over medium hot coals, for 8 to 10 minutes for medium rare. Place a small square of

Hot Bananas in the Skin

Place whole unpeeled bananas on the grill over medium hot coals. Cook, turning on both sides, for 8 minutes, or until hot throughout and the skin color has turned black. Serve with butter and a wedge of lime or lemon. Makes 2 servings.

Sautéed Chinese Peas

Wash ½ pound Chinese edible pea pods and break off the stem end. Put 1 tablespoon salad oil in a small disposable foil pan, add pods, and sauté over the barbecue coals for about 8 minutes, or until crisp-tender, turning occasionally. Makes 2 servings.

Strawberries de Luxe

1 box strawberries
¼ cup light brown sugar
½ cup sour cream
   Light brown sugar

Wash, hull, and halve or slice strawberries. Turn into a bowl and sprinkle with 3 tablespoons of the brown sugar. Gently stir in sour cream and sprinkle with the remaining tablespoon sugar. Chill at least 1 hour. Spoon into serving dishes and sprinkle with additional brown sugar. Makes 2 to 3 servings.

Menu

Chateaubriand of Beef
Sautéed Mushrooms
Asparagus with Cashew Butter
Green Salad   French Rolls
Crème de Menthe Sherbet

This meal requires no long preparation, but it keeps the cook busy for a few minutes prior to serving time. You will need to buy a Chateaubriand steak, which is a thick slice of beef taken by lateral cut through the thickest part of the tenderloin, allowing ½ to ¾ pound per serving. (You can also use a New York strip, fillet, or sirloin tip.) Prepare salad greens and have a French dressing or oil and vinegar ready so you can dress and mix the salad at the table. Start cooking the asparagus just before you begin broiling the steak. Purchase hard French rolls and the Crème de Menthe sherbet (or substitute mint or lime sherbet).

Chateaubriand of Beef

1 steak for Chateaubriand, about 1½ to 2
   inches thick (1 to 1½ lbs.)
2 to 3 tablespoons butter, melted
¼ pound medium-sized mushrooms, washed
   and sliced
   Dash of salt
   Freshly ground pepper

Place the steak in your electric frying pan or other frying pan in the melted butter and sauté over medium-high to high heat about 5 minutes per side for a medium-rare steak. Remove the cooked meat to a small warm serving platter; keep warm. Add the sliced mushrooms to the same pan and sauté 3 to 5 minutes, turning and stirring occasionally with a fork. Season with salt to taste. Spoon the cooked mushrooms and pan juices over the steak, and carve into two servings at the table. Pass a pepper grinder so that each serving can be seasoned to taste with freshly ground pepper. Makes 2 servings.

Asparagus with Cashew Butter

1 pound fresh asparagus or 1 package (10 oz.)
   frozen asparagus spears
¼ cup butter
2 teaspoons lemon juice
¼ teaspoon marjoram
¼ cup salted cashews, broken in lengthwise
   halves

Cook asparagus in salted water until tender, about 12 minutes, or, if using the frozen asparagus, cook as directed on the package. Drain cooked spears and arrange on the serving dish. Meanwhile, melt the butter in a small pan; add lemon juice, marjoram, and cashews. Simmer over low heat for 2 minutes. Pour over the cooked asparagus and serve. Makes 2 or 3 servings.

Menu

Sherried Consommé
Chopped Watercress
Beef Curry Hurry-up
Salted Peanuts
Hot Sesame Rolls with Butter
Pineapple Slices
Gingered Sour Cream

When seasoned in the Far East manner, leftover roast with gravy becomes a colorful full-meal dish. (You can also use canned roast beef and canned gravy for the same recipe.)

To prepare this quick curry dinner, heat the oven for the rolls; cook the rice. Drain the pineapple slices and arrange them on two serving dishes; chill. Combine beef and gravy (recipe follows) and let simmer; add rice when cooked. Clean and prepare the vegetables for the curry, watercress for the soup, and coarsely chop about ½ cup salted peanuts to serve with the curry. Heat the rolls; simmer the consommé in a small saucepan, adding ¼ cup sherry. Combine remaining ingredients for the curry. Serve the sherried consommé in bouillon cups; garnish with chopped watercress. Follow with curry. Top the pineapple slices with dollops of sour cream mixed with ginger, and serve.

Beef Curry Hurry-up

1   cup quick-cooking rice
1   cup cut-up leftover roast beef
¾   to 1 cup leftover gravy
1   teaspoon curry powder
½   bunch (about 5) green onions and tops, chopped
½   small green pepper, seeded and coarsely chopped
2   small tomatoes, peeled and cut in wedges
1   tablespoon soy sauce

Cook rice according to package directions until tender and fluffy (or use 1 cup leftover cooked rice). In a frying pan, heat the beef in gravy with curry powder. Stir in the steamed rice, chopped green onions, chopped pepper, tomatoes, and soy sauce, stirring carefully. Cook 2 or 3 minutes, just until heated through. Makes 2 servings.

Menu

Crisp Green Salad
Rack of Lamb
Mushroom-Onion Skewers
Fresh Peas in Patty Shells
Wheat Pilaf
Pound Cake à la Mode

One cut of meat that serves just two is rack of lamb. It's often a featured item on the menus of fine restaurants and consists of about eight lamb chops before they're cut apart. Eight lamb chops may sound like a lot, but the meat portion in each chop is small.

Make the salad ahead and chill; dress it just before serving. While the rack of lamb roasts, you'll have time to cook the pilaf and the peas, and assemble the mushroom-onion skewers, ready to put in the oven for the last 10 minutes with the meat. Bake frozen puff patty shells according to directions on the box.

Rack of Lamb

Purchase a Frenched rack of lamb (meat removed from the ends of the chop bones), with about 8 ribs, and have your meatman crack the loin bones. You might ask him for the paper frills to garnish the chops after the meat is cooked. Sprinkle the meat with ¼ teaspoon freshly ground pepper and lay in a small roasting pan with the rib bones pointing downward and fat side up. Combine ½ cup beef bouillon, ½ cup dry white cooking wine, and 1 clove garlic, mashed; use this mixture to baste the rack of lamb while it is cooking. Put into a hot oven (425°) and cook for 35 minutes (for rare) to 55 minutes (for well done). If you wish, insert meat thermometer into meat before cooking and cook until thermometer registers 170° to 180°.

While the meat is roasting, prepare the onion-mushroom skewers (directions follow) and put into oven with the meat during the last 10 minutes of cooking. To serve, arrange meat on platter with skewers; cap bone ends with paper frills, and cut rack into portions of 4 ribs each. Makes 2 servings.

Mushroom-Onion Skewers

Sauté 6 large mushrooms in 2 tablespoons butter over medium heat until shiny and dark. Drain 1 small can (8 oz.) small white onions and slip onto skewers alternately with the mushrooms. Put into oven with the lamb and cook for 10 minutes to heat through. Sprinkle with salt and pepper to taste.

Wheat Pilaf

1 tablespoon butter
1 tablespoon minced onion
½ cup bulgur or quick-cooking cracked wheat
1 cup beef bouillon
2 tablespoons minced parsley
Salt to taste

Melt the butter in a pan over medium heat, add onion and bulgur, and cook until onion is tender.

Stir in the bouillon and parsley; cover, and simmer about 15 minutes or until liquid is absorbed. Add salt to taste, dot with additional butter, if desired, and serve. Makes 2 servings.

Menu

Chopped Spinach and
Crumbled Bacon Salad
Lamb Chop Stew in Foil Packets
Hot Gingerbread
Kumquat Sauce and Sour Cream

Although this is a simple dinner to prepare, it takes several hours to bake. It is especially appropriate when you must be away from home before the dinner hour. You can put the gingerbread (made from a mix) into the oven to bake just before dinner, or make it ahead and reheat to serve.

Chopped Spinach and Crumbled Bacon Salad

Pick out the tender leaves from 1 bunch fresh spinach. Wash thoroughly and drain. Slice spinach in shreds and transfer to a bowl. Crumble in 2 crisp cooked slices of bacon (left over from breakfast) and 1 tablespoon grated Parmesan cheese. When ready to serve, pour over French dressing and toss lightly. Makes 2 servings.

Lamb Chop Stew in Foil Packets

For each serving, place on a large square of heavy metal foil 1 large shoulder lamb chop, 1 small potato, 1 small scraped carrot, 1 small peeled onion, ½ green pepper (optional), and a 3-inch celery stick. Sprinkle with salt and pepper and spoon over 1½ tablespoons sherry. Fold foil in a drugstore wrap. Place on a baking sheet, and bake in a moderate oven (350°) for about 2½ hours or until vegetables are tender.

Hot Gingerbread with Kumquat Sauce and Sour Cream

Bake a gingerbread mix as directed on the package. While the cake is warm, cut it in squares and top with a sauce made by slicing canned kumquats and heating them with some of their syrup and enough orange juice to thin it to a saucelike consistency. Spoon on a dollop of sour cream.

Menu

Sausage and Macaroni Casserole
Pickled Mushrooms with Tomatoes
Bread Sticks
Applesauce Crisp

You can keep the ingredients for this attractive casserole on hand indefinitely, ready to whip together in a few minutes. Use regular or French cut green beans, frozen or canned. If you like, mix another can of Vienna sausages with the macaroni and cheese. The dessert can be baked as you eat supper, or can be made ahead and served cold. It is made from canned apple sauce.

Sausage and Macaroni Casserole

1 can (about 15 oz.) macaroni in cheese sauce
1 package (10 oz.) frozen green beans, cooked and drained
1 teaspoon prepared mustard
1 can (4 oz.) Vienna sausages, drained
2 tablespoons grated Parmesan cheese

Spoon macaroni and cheese around the edge of a shallow 8-inch casserole (or pie pan). Mix beans with mustard and place in center of macaroni. Arrange sausages on macaroni; sprinkle with grated cheese. Bake, uncovered, in a moderate oven (350°) for 15 minutes or until thoroughly heated. Makes 2 to 3 servings.

Pickled Mushrooms with Tomatoes

Combine 1 jar (3½ oz.) whole pickled mushrooms and oil with 2 large peeled tomatoes, cut in slender wedges, and 1 or 2 tablespoons red wine vinegar. Chill and serve. Makes 3 servings.

Applesauce Crisp

Pour 1 can (about 1 lb.) apple sauce or 1½ to 2 cups canned or freshly made apple sauce (sweetened) into a shallow greased baking pan and dust top lightly with nutmeg; sprinkle with ¼ cup raisins and ⅔ cup crushed zwieback crumbs. Dot crumbs with 3 tablespoons butter or margarine. Bake in a moderately hot oven (375°) for 20 minutes. Makes 3 or 4 servings.

Menu

Lemon-Glazed Pork Chops
Golden Potato Patties
Basil-Topped Tomatoes
Green Salad with Cucumbers
French Dressing
Hot Buttered French Bread
Broiled Pears with Currant Jelly

Use your broiler to prepare this dinner for two or three people. Slow broiling gives the thinly cut pork chops time to cook thoroughly without charring. Add a generous amount of diced cucumbers to your favorite salad greens and mix with French dressing. The buttered French bread, wrapped in foil, heats beneath the broiler pan or in the oven.

Lemon-Glazed Pork Chops

Preheat the broiler. Allow 1 or 2 chops per person. Score thin pork chops and broil 3 or 4 inches from heat until well browned; season with salt and pepper, then broil other side. Spoon lemon glaze (recipe to follow) over each chop; top with a thin lemon slice and return to broiler until glaze bubbles and browns slightly.

Lemon Glaze:

Blend 2 to 3 teaspoons prepared mustard, ½ teaspoon grated lemon peel, and 1 tablespoon lemon juice with ½ cup firmly packed brown sugar.

Golden Potato Patties

Broil 1 package (about 12 oz.) frozen potato patties along with chops. Baste with melted butter occasionally. Top patties with foil if they reach desired brown color before chops are cooked.

Basil-Topped Tomatoes

Brush thick slices of tomatoes with melted butter. Season with salt and a sprinkle of basil. Put under broiler for a quick heating-up when you add glaze to the pork chops.

Broiled Pears with Currant Jelly

Cut winter pears in half, peel, and remove cores; brush each half with melted butter. Place pear halves, cut side down, on a broiler rack and broil 5 minutes. Turn pears over, dot with butter, and continue broiling 5 minutes. Fill the hollow of each pear half with currant jelly. Serve warm.

Swordfish Steak with Lemon Baste

Dip both sides of two ¾-inch-thick swordfish steaks (about ½ pound each) into a mixture of ¼ cup melted butter or margarine, juice of ½ lemon, 1 tablespoon minced parsley, and ½ teaspoon salt. Grill about 8 inches above hot coals for about 7 minutes per side, basting once during cooking. Makes 2 servings.

Zucchini-Tomato Kebabs

Parboil 2 medium-sized zucchini for 4 to 5 minutes in about 2 cups salted water seasoned with ½ teaspoon oregano. Remove and cut each crosswise in 4 sections. Thread alternately with cherry tomatoes on 2 small skewers. Baste with melted butter and cook about 8 inches above coals on a grill for about 10 minutes, turning and basting frequently. Just before removing from grill, sprinkle each kebab with 1 tablespoon Parmesan cheese and a dash of salt and pepper. Serve immediately. Makes 2 servings.

Rice Pilaf Salad

½ cup quick-cooking brown rice
¾ cup boiling water
1 chicken bouillon cube
3 tablespoons mayonnaise
3 tablespoons chopped canned mushrooms
2 tablespoons lemon juice
¼ teaspoon thyme
¼ teaspoon curry powder
   Lettuce

Add rice to boiling water with bouillon cube. Reduce heat, cover, and steam for 15 minutes. Chill. Make dressing by combining mayonnaise, mushrooms, lemon juice, thyme, and curry. Mix with chilled rice and arrange on lettuce-lined salad plates. Makes 2 servings.

Barbecued swordfish with a lemon baste and zucchini-tomato kebabs make the entrée for this outdoor dinner.

Menu

Swordfish Steak with Lemon Baste
Zucchini-Tomato Kebabs
Rice Pilaf Salad
Rye Wafers
Cantaloupe   Fresh Strawberry Sauce

A small barbecue grill on the patio will take care of both hot dishes in this simple but elegant meal. The rye wafers come from the market.

You can prepare the simple baste for the swordfish and thread the skewers with the vegetables either just before grilling or several hours in advance (refrigerate). Cook rice for the salad in time to chill it before adding dressing. Prepare and refrigerate the cantaloupe dessert at least an hour in advance.

Cantaloupe with Fresh Strawberry Sauce

Whirl in a blender or mash ½ cup fresh strawberries with 2 tablespoons sugar and 1½ tablespoons lemon juice. Pour sauce into two prepared halves of a small cantaloupe; cover and chill in refrigerator until serving time (at least 1 hour). Makes 2 servings.

Menu

Lobster Newburg
Cheese Patty Shells
Fresh Orange Slices on Watercress
Broccoli with Buttered Almonds
Cheesecake with Boysenberries or
Blueberries in Syrup

This quite elegant meal for two is simple to prepare. Everything but the orange salad comes straight from the freezer.

Lobster Newburg

Heat 1 package (11½ oz.) frozen lobster Newburg as directed on the package, or prepare this quick version: Add 1 to 2 cups sliced rock lobster tail meat to 1 can (10 oz.) white sauce and heat gently, stirring until simmering. Turn heat low. Beat two egg yolks and blend with some of the sauce, and return to pan. Stir in 1½ tablespoons sherry or Madeira, and salt and pepper to taste; remove from heat. Spoon mixture into cheese patty shells (recipe follows) and top with the patty shell lids. Makes 2 servings.

Cheese Patty Shells

Bake 4 frozen puff patty shells according to directions on the box. Remove centers as directed. Sprinkle shells and lids with ¼ cup shredded Swiss cheese. Return to oven long enough to melt cheese.

Broccoli with Buttered Almonds

Cook 1 package (10 oz.) frozen broccoli spears according to directions on the box. Lightly brown 2 tablespoons sliced almonds in 1 tablespoon butter or margarine. Drain broccoli and pour the butter and almond mixture over it and serve. Makes 2 servings.

Cheesecake with Boysenberries or Blueberries in Syrup

Thaw a frozen cheesecake and serve slices topped with partially thawed boysenberries or blueberries in sugar syrup.

For a hearty supper, serve this Scottish soup-stew. Accompaniments are oatmeal bread, Swiss and Gouda cheeses, and lettuce wedges with dressing. Recipe on page 60.

Family and Company Suppers

Quite often you need a light meal to serve your family or guests. This need may arise when the weather is warm and appetites are low, during busy weekday nights, or on week ends when family or friends have returned from an evening's entertainment. Light suppers are especially welcome at teen-age gatherings.

Some of the supper menus that follow are most suitable as family meals, while others are fancy enough for informal entertaining. Some require advance preparation, and others can be put together before the eyes of your family or guests. The introduction following each menu will tell you just what occasion that particular menu best suits and how best to serve it—from the coffee table, around the fireplace, from the electric frying pan on the dining-room table, on the run, or out on the patio.

Menu

Sherry Clam Chowder

Sour Cream Topping

Crisp Green Salad

Oil and Vinegar Dressing

Bread Sticks

Blueberry Buckle   Lemon Ice Cream

Clam chowder doesn't demand the accompaniment of many courses for supper—just a crisp green salad, bread sticks, and a grand dessert. This old-fashioned Blueberry Buckle is as satisfying made with frozen blueberries as it is with fresh ones. Don't compromise on richness, but serve it warm with generous proportions of lemon ice cream alongside. You might roll out a few bread sticks between your palms and bake them when you make yeast bread; keep in your freezer, or buy them for this menu.

Sherry Clam Chowder

8 slices bacon, cut in small pieces
2 medium-sized onions, chopped
2 cups chopped celery
2 cans (about 10 oz. each) frozen potato soup
1 bottle (8 oz.) clam juice, or 1 cup nectar
1 soup can of milk
2 cans (about 7 oz. each) minced clams with
  nectar (or 1 cup chopped steamed clams
    and ½ cup nectar)
3 tablespoons sherry
6 large spoonfuls sour cream

In a large frying pan, cook bacon, onions, and celery until vegetables are tender. In a saucepan, heat frozen potato soup with clam juice and milk.

Add sautéed bacon, onions, and celery. Heat just to boiling. Add minced clams with nectar. Heat through. Stir in sherry. Ladle into soup bowls. Top each with a spoonful of sour cream. Makes 6 servings.

Blueberry Buckle

¼ cup (⅛ lb.) butter or margarine
½ cup sugar
1 egg
1 teaspoon vanilla
1 cup sifted regular all-purpose flour
1 teaspoon baking powder
¼ teaspoon salt
⅓ cup milk
  About 2 cups fresh or frozen unsweetened
  blueberries
½ cup sugar
⅓ cup unsifted regular all-purpose flour
½ teaspoon cinnamon
⅛ teaspoon nutmeg
¼ cup (⅛ lb.) butter or margarine

Cream together ¼ cup butter and ½ cup sugar. Beat in egg and vanilla. Sift flour with baking powder and salt. Add sifted dry ingredients to creamed mixture alternately with milk, beginning and ending with dry ingredients. Turn into a greased shallow baking pan (9 inches square or about 8 by 10 inches). Cover cake batter evenly with blueberries. Combine ½ cup sugar, ⅓ cup flour, cinnamon, and nutmeg. With pastry blender, cut ¼ cup butter into flour mixture until crumbly. Sprinkle crumbled mixture evenly over blueberries. Bake in a moderately hot oven (375°) for 40 to 45 minutes. Set pan on wire rack to cool slightly. Makes 6 to 8 servings.

Menu

Hotch-Potch
Sliced Cheeses
Oatmeal Bread
Lettuce Wedges
Sour Cream Dressing
Gingerbread with Lemon Sauce

When appetites are hearty, this Scottish soup-stew is satisfying. It is chock-full of vegetables, but has a thin, well-seasoned broth.

You can make the hotch-potch ahead and reheat it when you are ready to serve. Offer a selection of cheeses with the oatmeal bread. Cut a crisp head of lettuce in wedges and serve with your favorite sour cream dressing. For dessert, make ginger-bread from a prepared mix or your favorite recipe; cut it in squares and serve with Tart Lemon Sauce.

Hotch-Potch

8   cups water
1   pound lamb neck slices
2   teaspoons salt
1   teaspoon pepper
1   cup sliced carrots (about 2 medium-sized)
1   cup sliced turnips
1   medium-sized onion, chopped
1   cup chopped raw cauliflower
1   package (10 oz.) frozen peas
1   package (10 oz.) frozen green beans
½   head lettuce, cut in thin strips

Pour water into 4-quart pan and add lamb, salt, and pepper. Bring to a boil over high heat. Reduce heat and skim. Simmer 2 hours or until meat is tender. Add carrots, turnips, and onion; bring to

boil again and cook 20 minutes or until vegetables are tender-crisp. Add cauliflower, peas, green beans, and lettuce, and bring to a boil again; cook 5 minutes. Remove lamb bones. Serve hot in large soup bowls. Makes 6 generous servings.

Tart Lemon Sauce

In a small saucepan, melt ½ cup butter or mar-garine. Remove from heat and add 1 cup sugar, ⅔ cup lemon juice, and 2 eggs, well beaten. Mix until well blended. Cook, stirring, over medium heat until smooth and thickened. Makes 1 cup.

Menu

Pimiento Cream Soup
Crisp Salted Crackers
Pine-Apple Dumplings

Warn the family to save room for warm, pineapple-glazed apple dumplings before you serve them bowls of steaming soup. The soup is an unusual and delicious combination of spaghetti and pi-miento in an egg-rich stock base. Make the dessert first; while it bakes, you can make the soup.

Pimiento Cream Soup

1 cup spaghetti (uncooked)
1 cup minced celery
4 cups boiling chicken or beef broth (canned or made from chicken or beef stock base)
1 tablespoon minced onion
6 canned pimientos, minced (approximately 2 cans of 4-oz. size)
2 egg yolks
½ cup light cream
  Salt and pepper to taste

Add spaghetti and celery to chicken or beef broth. Cover and simmer 20 minutes. Add onion and pimientos. Beat together egg yolks and light cream. Add some of the hot stock to egg mixture; then add egg mixture to soup, stirring constantly. Season with salt and pepper. Keep soup hot to serve, but do not boil. Makes 4 to 6 servings.

Pine-Apple Dumplings

  Pastry for a 2-crust pie
6 apples, peeled and cored
  Ready-mix cinnamon-sugar
3 teaspoons butter or margarine

Syrup:

1 can (9 oz.) pineapple slices, cut up, and syrup (or use 4 slices canned pineapple and ½ cup of the syrup)
1 cup brown sugar, firmly packed
½ cup granulated sugar
1 cup red wine
½ cup hot water
4 tablespoons butter or margarine

Roll out pastry on a lightly floured board and cut out six 6-inch squares. Place each apple on a square of pastry. Fill cores with ready-mix cinnamon-sugar. Dot each apple with ½ teaspoon butter or margarine. To seal dumplings, bring corners of pastry over apple and pinch edges shut. Arrange in a baking pan (choose one with a 2-inch rim) and pour over hot syrup (directions follow). Bake in a hot oven (400°) for 25 minutes or until apples are done and dumplings are brown; baste frequently. Serve hot. Makes 6 servings.

To make syrup, combine the cut-up pineapple slices and pineapple syrup with brown sugar, granulated sugar, red wine, hot water, and 4 tablespoons butter or margarine; boil for 5 minutes.

Menu

Fresh Tomato Soup
Cheddar Cheese Bread
Fresh Grape Clusters

It takes only minutes to prepare this aromatic, golden cheese bread, made with biscuit mix. While it bakes, you have plenty of time to make the fresh tomato soup. For dessert, snip bunches of fresh grapes that are in season.

Fresh tomato soup and hot Cheddar cheese bread, fresh from the oven, make a satisfying supper.

Fresh Tomato Soup

2 tablespoons butter or margarine
4 green onions, thinly sliced (including tops)
1 cup thinly sliced okra
4 large tomatoes, peeled and diced
2 cups chicken broth
1½ tablespoons lemon juice
2 teaspoons sugar
   Salt and pepper to taste

Melt butter or margarine in a saucepan; add onions, okra, and tomatoes; cover and simmer about 5 minutes. Add chicken broth, lemon juice, sugar, salt, and pepper. Bring to a boil and simmer 5 to 10 minutes. Makes 4 to 5 servings.

Cheddar Cheese Bread

3¾ cups biscuit mix
¾ cup shredded sharp Cheddar cheese
6 slices bacon, cooked and crumbled
1 egg
1½ cups buttermilk

Mix biscuit mix with Cheddar cheese and bacon. Beat egg with buttermilk. Combine with biscuit mix and stir just until blended. Pour into a well greased 5 by 9-inch loaf pan. Bake in a moderate oven (350°) for 1 hour. Serve warm.

Menu

Tomato Supper Sandwich
Coleslaw
Chilled Melon

Simple but hearty, this easy family supper features a robust sandwich of corned beef, tomatoes, and cheese on a biscuit base.

First prepare the supper sandwich. While it is baking, make the cole slaw from your favorite recipe or use a commercial dressing. For dessert, choose your favorite melon and have it well chilled.

Tomato Supper Sandwich

1½ cups sifted regular all-purpose flour
3 teaspoons baking powder
½ teaspoon seasoned salt
¼ cup mayonnaise
⅓ cup milk
1 can (12 oz.) chilled corned beef, cut in thin slices
   Prepared mustard
   Mayonnaise
   Tomatoes, thinly sliced
   Cheddar cheese, thinly sliced

First prepare a biscuit oblong by sifting flour with baking powder and seasoned salt. Mix ¼ cup mayonnaise with milk; carefully stir into sifted ingredients. On a lightly floured board, roll dough into an oblong about ¼ inch thick. Place on a baking sheet.

Arrange corned beef to cover biscuit dough. Spread lightly with prepared mustard and mayonnaise. Cover with tomato slices; top with Cheddar cheese slices. Bake in a hot oven (425°) for 15 to 20 minutes, or until the biscuit base is golden brown. Cut in serving-size squares; serve hot. Makes 6 servings.

Menu

Lettuce and Asparagus Salad
Egg-Steak Sandwich
Pineapple Bars
Vanilla Ice Cream

A hot steak and egg sandwich and a crisp green salad can be an impressive late supper when you have to prepare a meal on short notice. Preparation will take you no more than 20 minutes. Make the pineapple bars if you have time, or buy cookies.

Egg-Steak Sandwich

Oval-shaped French bread slices
Butter
Oval-shaped frozen cube steaks
Eggs
Smoke-flavored salt
Coarse-ground pepper

Spread 1 slice of bread for each sandwich generously with butter, place under the broiler, and heat through. Meanwhile, sauté the meat (one steak per sandwich) in butter as directed on the package. At the same time, in a separate frying pan, fry the same number of eggs to your own taste. Assemble each sandwich by placing a cooked steak on a warm bread slice; then top each steak with a fried egg. Sprinkle the smoke-flavored salt and the pepper over the egg. Serve the sandwich immediately, providing a knife and fork.

Lettuce and Asparagus Salad

Iceberg or romaine lettuce
Canned asparagus spears (one 10-oz. can is
    sufficient for 4 salads)
Tarragon French dressing (recipe follows)
Paprika

For each salad you will need about 1 cup torn iceberg or romaine lettuce and ⅓ to ½ cup inch-long pieces of drained, canned asparagus spears (or leftover cooked fresh asparagus). Arrange the lettuce in individual salad bowls; scatter the asparagus pieces over the top. Dress salad with the tarragon French dressing (recipe follows) and sprinkle paprika over the top of the salad.

Tarragon French Dressing:

Combine ⅓ cup tarragon vinegar with ¼ teaspoon salt in a small jar or shaker. Add about ⅔ cup olive oil or salad oil; shake or stir just before putting required amount over the individual salads. Makes 1 cup dressing.

Pineapple Bars

  1 cup regular all-purpose flour (sift before
    measuring)
  1 teaspoon baking powder
 ½ cup (¼ lb.) butter or margarine
  2 eggs
  1 tablespoon milk
  1 can (about 1 lb., 4 oz.) crushed pineapple
 ¼ cup melted butter
  1 cup sugar
  1 cup flaked coconut
  1 teaspoon vanilla

Sift flour with baking powder. With pastry blender, cut in ½ cup butter or margarine until mixture is crumbly. Beat 1 egg with the milk; stir into flour mixture. Spread over bottom of 8-inch-square baking pan. Thoroughly drain can of crushed pineapple and spread over top. Beat remaining 1 egg thoroughly; stir in melted butter, sugar, flaked coconut, and vanilla. Spread this topping over pineapple. Bake in a moderate oven (350°) for 35 to 40 minutes. Cool and cut into about 16 squares.

Menu

Hot Meatball Sandwiches
Cucumber Sticks, Green Pepper Rings,
Ripe Olives, Dill Pickles
Easy Coconut-Topped Cake
Milk or Iced Tea

Here is a supper for a Saturday or Sunday night gathering of teen-agers. The meal is an eat-with-the-fingers affair. But you can provide dessert forks if you prefer.

Tiny meatballs in a thick tomato sauce fill the hot sandwiches. These are messy, so use big napkins or bandanas, bib-style, as a shield for any filling that might spill. Make the relishes in advance and crisp them in ice water. The cake, with its broiled topping, can be served warm from the oven or at room temperature.

Hearty meatball sandwiches, made with French rolls, are finger food—but provide bibs to catch spills.

Hot Meatball Sandwiches

1½ pounds ground lean beef
½ pound ground lean pork
 2 eggs
½ cup fine dry bread crumbs
½ cup grated Romano cheese
¼ cup chopped parsley
½ teaspoon salt
 1 package (1½ oz.) spaghetti sauce mix
   with mushrooms·
 1 tablespoon butter or margarine
 1 can (8 oz.) tomato sauce
½ cup water
 8 round French rolls
   Butter or margarine
   Grated Romano cheese

Thoroughly mix meats, eggs, crumbs, the ½ cup cheese, parsley, salt, and half the dry sauce mix (about 2 tablespoons). Using a rounded tablespoon for each, shape meat mixture into 1½-inch balls. Brown meatballs in the 1 tablespoon butter in a large frying pan that has a cover; shake pan to brown meatballs on all sides. Remove meatballs from pan and keep warm. Discard fat. In the same pan, prepare the remaining sauce mix by blending it with tomato sauce and water; heat until bubbly. Return meatballs to pan, cover, and cook over low heat about 25 minutes. Split and butter rolls; wrap in foil and heat in a moderate oven (350°) for about 15 minutes. Serve meatballs in rolls, allowing 5 to 6 meatballs and a spoonful of sauce for each. Sprinkle with additional cheese. Makes 8 sandwiches.

Easy Coconut-Topped Cake

 2 eggs, slightly beaten
 1 cup sugar
 1 cup regular all-purpose flour (sift before
   measuring)
 1 teaspoon baking powder
½ teaspoon salt
½ cup milk
 3 tablespoons butter or margarine
¼ teaspoon vanilla
   Coconut topping (recipe follows)

Gradually add to the slightly beaten eggs the sugar, beating constantly, until mixture is very thick and light. Sift flour again with baking powder and salt; blend the flour mixture into the egg mixture. Scald the milk; add butter or margarine and vanilla; stir until butter is melted. Blend milk mixture into the flour mixture. Spread batter in a well-greased 9-inch square pan. Bake in a moderate oven (350°) for 20 to 25 minutes or until cake tests done and is golden brown. Remove from oven, cool slightly, spread with Coconut Topping (recipe follows), and place under the broiler for several minutes until lightly browned and bubbly. Cut in bars or squares. Makes about 9 servings.

Coconut Topping:

Melt ⅓ cup butter or margarine in a small pan. Remove from heat and mix in ¾ cup firmly packed brown sugar, 2 tablespoons light cream, and 2 cups shredded fresh or packaged coconut until well blended.

Menu

Corn Chip Chili
Lettuce Wedges
Your Favorite Dressing
Bowl of Corn Chips
Baked Macaroon Pears

This menu is made from foods that may be kept on hand for an emergency. The chili casserole can be prepared in advance and heated just before serving. The dessert will bake at the same time as the casserole. Lettuce wedges with your favorite homemade or commercial dressing and a bowl of corn chips round out the meal.

Corn Chip Chili

  3 cans (15 oz. each) red kidney beans, drained
  2 cans (about 10 oz. each) enchilada sauce
  2 cups shredded Cheddar cheese
1½ tablespoons chili powder
  1 package (6 oz.) corn chips
1½ pounds ground beef chuck
  1 to 2 tablespoons salad oil (optional)
1½ cups chopped onions
  1 clove garlic, minced
    About 1 cup sour cream

Combine kidney beans, enchilada sauce, Cheddar cheese, chili powder, and corn chips. Cook ground chuck in salad oil (if needed) with onions and garlic, until meat is brown and the onions tender. Stir together the meat and bean mixtures; pour into a 3-quart baking dish. Bake, uncovered, in a moderate oven (350°) for about 30 minutes, until hot and bubbly. Remove from oven; top with dollops of sour cream. Return chili to oven; heat 5 minutes more. Makes 8 to 10 servings.

Baked Macaroon Pears

Using 2 cans (1 lb., 14 oz. each) pear halves, cut halves into ½-inch slices; drain, reserving ¼ cup of the syrup. Heat the syrup with 2 tablespoons apricot preserves; pour over pears. Sprinkle pears with ½ cup dry macaroon crumbs; dot with 1 tablespoon butter. Bake in a moderate oven (350°) about 20 minutes, until crumbs are browned. Serve warm, plain, or with ice cream. Makes 4 servings.

Menu

Cantaloupe Curry with Condiments
Crisp Bread Sticks
Lime Sherbet

This savory chicken curry is served in individual cantaloupe half-shells, each surrounded by lettuce-cup condiment dishes. With it, offer crisp little bread sticks and a fruit sherbet dessert. Prepare the condiments first, then start the curry.

Cantaloupe Curry

Cut 2 room-temperature cantaloupes in half; remove seeds. With grapefruit knife, enlarge cavity if necessary to about ½-cup size. If you wish, cut the removed melon in bite-size pieces and add to the curry. Fill the melon center with Quick Chicken Curry (recipe follows). Top each with a small mound of hot rice mixed with sliced green onion tops.

Quick Chicken Curry:

    1 tablespoon butter
    ½ teaspoon curry powder
    ½ teaspoon seasoned salt
    1 tablespoon lemon juice
    3 tablespoons finely chopped green onions
    1 can (10½ oz.) white sauce
    1½ cups diced cooked chicken (turkey, small
       shrimp, crab meat, or lobster may be used)

In a saucepan, heat together until bubbly the butter and curry powder. Add seasoned salt, lemon juice, chopped green onions, and white sauce; heat. Add cooked chicken. Heat to boiling. Makes 4 servings.

Supper entreé is cantaloupe curry in individual servings surrounded by condiments in lettuce cups.

Curry Condiments:

Offer sautéed raisins (sauté light or dark raisins in a little melted butter; sprinkle lightly with seasoned salt), chopped peanuts mixed with toasted flaked coconut, pitted dates marinated in French dressing, tiny whole tomatoes, and stuffed green olives.

Menu

Beef Tacos
Green Salad
Pineapple Sherbet

For this meal, set the table with all the makings of both tacos and salad and let each person assemble his own, choosing from greens, vegetables, and relishes. This gives a wide choice for all ages in the family and allows the children to avoid any hotness they may object to in Mexican food.

You can make the beef taco filling ahead of time. Just before serving, fry the tortillas until slightly crisp; fold and fill them with the beef.

Prepare the table by making an arrangement of the taco and salad makings: a salad bowl of 1 small head of shredded iceberg lettuce; a large platter filled with wedges of 2 tomatoes, 1 sliced cucumber, wedges of 2 hard-cooked eggs, about ½ cup chopped ripe olives, 1 green pepper cut in narrow rings, and about ¾ cup chopped green onions; a small bowl filled with 1 cup shredded sharp Cheddar cheese; bottles of chili sauce, catsup, taco sauce, pickle relish, and French dressing; and the beef-filled tortillas.

Beef Tacos

    1   pound ground beef
    1   medium-sized onion, finely chopped
1½   teaspoons chili powder
    ½   teaspoon oregano
    ½   teaspoon paprika
    ¼   teaspoon rosemary
    ¼   teaspoon pepper
    1   teaspoon salt
    3   tablespoons taco sauce
    2   teaspoons Worcestershire

Brown meat until crumbly; add onion, chili powder, oregano, paprika, rosemary, pepper, salt,

taco sauce, and Worcestershire. Blend well and heat through.

Tortillas:

Fry 8 to 10 tortillas, one at a time, in about ⅛-inch of salad oil in a large frying pan over high heat for about 30 seconds on each side, or until slightly crisp. Fold in half as you remove from pan; drain on paper towels. Fill each folded taco with about 2 tablespoons of beef filling; keep warm until all are made. At table, add lettuce, tomatoes, and other vegetables. Makes 4 to 5 servings.

Menu

Eggs Mornay
Rice Muffins
Fresh Apple Pie
Assorted Nuts in Shells

Here is an easy-to-assemble meal for a busy schedule. Swiss cheese and Parmesan cheese give a piquant flavor to the hard-cooked eggs.

You might have the eggs cooked ahead before supper. Make the muffins; while they bake, you can assemble the main dish.

Heat egg dish under the broiler just before bringing it to the table. Use your favorite recipe for the apple pie or buy a frozen or bakery pie.

Eggs Mornay

12 hard-cooked eggs
 1 small can (about 4 oz.) liver pâté
 3 cups thin cream sauce (3 cups milk,
   3 tablespoons flour, 3 tablespoons butter)
   Salt and pepper
½ cup shredded Swiss cheese
½ cup grated Parmesan cheese

Cut eggs in half lengthwise. Remove yolks and blend together with the liver pâté; stir in 2 table-spoons of the cream sauce and salt and pepper to taste. Stuff eggs with the egg yolk mixture; arrange eggs in a shallow baking dish. Add the Swiss cheese and half of the Parmesan cheese to the re-maining cream sauce. Stirring, cook over low heat until cheese melts. Pour sauce over eggs; sprinkle with the remaining Parmesan. Heat under the broiler until bubbly and brown. Makes 6 servings.

Rice Muffins

  2 egg yolks, well beaten
1¼ cups milk
  3 tablespoons melted butter
  1 cup cooked rice
1½ cups sifted regular all-purpose flour
 ½ teaspoon salt
  2 teaspoons baking powder
  1 tablespoon sugar
    Pinch of nutmeg
  2 egg whites

Stir egg yolks into milk, melted butter, and cooked rice. Sift flour with salt, baking powder, sugar, and nutmeg. Add dry ingredients to egg yolk mixture, and stir just until all the flour is moistened. Beat egg whites until stiff; fold into flour mixture. Pour into 18 large greased muffin cups; bake in a moderately hot oven (425°) for 25 minutes, or until golden brown. Makes 18 muffins.

Menu

Fruit Salad in Romaine Leaves with
Mint Dressing
Cold Cuts   Assorted Breads
Ice Cream
Cinnamon Crisps

An attractive fruit salad, served with assorted cold cuts and breads is the basis of this light but sustain-ing supper. Romaine lettuce leaves are containers for the individual salad, which you can arrange on a platter to serve with such cold cuts as sliced ham, tongue, and roast beef.

Fruit Salad in Romaine Leaves

  1 pint country style cottage cheese
 ¼ teaspoon seasoned salt
  3 tablespoons mayonnaise
 ½ cup coarsely chopped pecans, cashews,
    or walnuts
1½ cups cut-up fruit or whole berries
    (cantaloupe or honeydew melon, fresh
    peaches, grapes, strawberries)
  6 well-shaped, medium-sized romaine leaves

Combine cottage cheese, seasoned salt, and mayonnaise. Gently stir in nuts and fruit. Spoon the fruit and cheese mixture into the 6 romaine leaves. Arrange each filled leaf on a large platter. Serve with Mint Dressing (recipe follows). Makes 6 servings.

Mint Dressing:

½ cup mint jelly
¼ cup salad oil
¼ teaspoon grated lime peel
 2 or 3 tablespoons lime juice
   Few grains salt

Beat the mint jelly with a rotary beater until smooth. Add salad oil, grated lime peel, lime juice, and salt. Stir until blended. Makes about ¾ cup dressing.

Cinnamon Crisps

    1 package (9 oz.) refrigerated cinnamon rolls
       Melted butter
    1 cup sugar
    2 to 3 tablespoons cinnamon
    ¼ cup chopped nuts

Dip each roll, cinnamon side down, into melted butter. Have ready a mixture of the sugar, cinnamon, and chopped nuts on a board. Set each roll in the sugar mixture, buttered side down, and roll until it is about ⅛ inch thick. Turn the sugar side up and bake on a well greased baking sheet in a hot oven (400°) for 10 minutes, or until brown and bubbling. Serve hot or cold. Makes 8 crisps.

Menu

Herbed Chicken Livers

Buttered Egg Noodles   Green Salad

Spiced Cherry Compote

Wafer Cookies

One reason restaurant menus offer sautéed dishes is that this cooking method is quick and easy. Sautéing offers the same advantages in home kitchens, as demonstrated by the savory chicken liver entrée in this menu.

Have the water hot and drop in the noodles as you start cooking the livers in order to have them ready to serve together. Mix the salad with a favorite dressing. It will take less than 30 minutes to prepare the entire meal.

Herbed Chicken Livers

    1 pound chicken livers, cut in halves
    3 tablespoons flour
    ½ teaspoon paprika
    ¼ teaspoon salt
    ¼ teaspoon pepper
 1½   tablespoons salad oil
 1½   tablespoons butter or margarine
    1 clove garlic, minced
    ½ medium-sized onion, finely chopped
    2 sprigs parsley, finely chopped
    ⅛ teaspoon minced or crumbled rosemary
    ½ pound medium-sized mushrooms,
       cut in quarters
    ⅛ teaspoon thyme
    1 teaspoon chicken stock base
    ½ cup dry white table wine

Toss chicken livers with mixture of flour, paprika, salt, and pepper. Heat salad oil and butter or margarine in frying pan; add livers and cook, stirring, until they begin to brown. Add garlic, onion, parsley, rosemary, and mushrooms. Sauté over high heat, stirring for about 2 minutes. Blend in thyme, chicken stock base, and dry white wine. Cover and simmer about 4 minutes or until the livers are done to your liking. Makes 4 servings.

Spiced Cherry Compote

    3 cans (1 lb. each) sour pitted cherries
       Water
 1½   cups sugar
    1 tablespoon cinnamon
    3 lemons, thinly sliced
 1½   teaspoons almond extract
       Few drops red food coloring

Drain the cherries. Save the liquid; measure and add water to make 2 cups. Combine liquid with sugar, cinnamon, and lemon slices (reserve a few lemon slices for garnish). Simmer, uncovered, until syrup is reduced one-half. Add almond extract, cherries, red food coloring, and remaining lemon slices. Heat through. Makes 8 to 10 servings.

Here's a steak dinner for guests: chilled berry soup, salad with Gorgonzola cheese, special beef steaks, fresh beans, potatoes, chocolate cream dessert. Recipes are on pages 78 and 79.

Small Dinner Parties

Food ideas that save time are especially valuable when you entertain. This chapter offers dinner menus that employ a variety of techniques to make entertaining easy, yet elegant.

Many of the meals can be made in advance so that the hostess needs only to heat and assemble them before serving. Other menus make use of such shortcuts as prepared mixes and frozen foods, which are especially convenient when you have

unexpected guests. Included also are buffets, an excellent means of serving people simply and quickly. Still another idea to make the hostess' job easier is a dinner designed for serving from a cart fitted with a warming tray. Some simple foods not usually considered company fare are given special treatment in several of the menus, thus creating dinners that are not only time-saving, but economical.

Menu

Mushroom Soup
Oven Sauté Chicken
Barley Pilaf
Tossed Greens Salad
Roquefort Dressing
Hot Buttered French Bread
West Indies Parfait with
Strawberries

This menu is well suited to easy entertaining. The chicken entrée and the barley pilaf, a nice change from rice or potatoes, cook together in the same oven. The creamy parfait dessert is one you can make early and let chill.

Try dehydrated mushroom soup to start this meal, giving the soup a freshly made effect by adding 1 teaspoon sherry to each cup and sprinkling each serving with minced parsley. The chicken cooks completely in the oven, but the pilaf is started on top of the range. Select a combination of greens and a favorite Roquefort dressing for the salad; make the parfaits early in the day.

Oven Sauté Chicken

Thinly slice 1 large onion; scatter over the bottom of a shallow baking pan. Coat with melted butter or margarine 2 whole chicken breasts, 3 or 4 thighs, or 3 or 4 legs. Place in a single layer over onions in baking pan. Sprinkle with paprika (about 2 or 3 tablespoons) and salt. Tuck in about 6 whole cloves of garlic (optional). Blend ¼ cup catsup with ½ cup Sauterne wine and pour into pan, but not over chicken pieces. Cover and bake in a moderate oven (350°) for 1 hour; remove cover last 15 minutes. Discard garlic; serve with pan juices. Makes 4 to 6 servings.

Barley Pilaf

Cover 1½ cups pearl barley with water and let stand 1 hour; drain. Cook in 4 cups salted boiling water just until tender, about 25 minutes. Drain, then rinse with cold water. Combine in a casserole 6 tablespoons lightly browned butter or margarine (browned with 2 whole cloves of garlic, if you wish), ¾ cup water, 1 crumbled chicken bouillon cube, 3 thinly sliced green onions (including tops), ⅓ cup minced parsley, and salt to taste. Cover tightly and bake along with the chicken in a moderate oven (350°) for 30 minutes. Makes 4 to 6 servings.

West Indies Parfait with Strawberries

1½ cups light cream
¼ cup butter or margarine
3 egg yolks
½ cup dark brown sugar, firmly packed
1 envelope unflavored gelatin
¼ cup water
   Dash of salt
¾ teaspoon rum flavoring (or rum to taste)
3 egg whites
¼ cup granulated sugar
   Strawberries, sliced and sugared

In the top of a double boiler, heat to scalding the light cream with butter or margarine. Beat egg yolks with dark brown sugar; blend in some of the hot mixture, then return all to double boiler. Cook over simmering water, stirring, until thickened. Soften gelatin in water; blend with hot mixture until dissolved. Flavor with salt and rum. Chill until softly set. Whip egg whites until stiff; gradually beat in granulated sugar until peaks are stiff and glossy. Fold into chilled mixture. Spoon into parfait glasses, making alternating layers of strawberries and parfait mixture; or reserve the berries to spoon on top later. Chill. Makes 6 servings.

The greens and reds of this easy party dinner make it especially suited to Christmastime entertaining.

Menu

Chicken-Sausage Turnovers

Limas with Lemon-Dill Butter

Avocado-Beet Salad

Sesame Wafers

Green Olives

Almonds

Eggnog Ice Cream

Nearly everything in this buffet menu is prepared in advance so you need only to heat and assemble a couple of dishes just prior to service.

The Chicken-Sausage Turnovers can be assembled in the morning and refrigerated until baking time, about 45 minutes before dinner, or you can bake them in the morning and reheat to serve. Make the gelatin mixture for the Avocado-Beet Salad several hours in advance and refrigerate; shortly before serving, spoon it into prepared avocado halves. While the limas cook, make the seasoned butter to pour over them. Sesame wafers can be purchased at the grocery store or delicatessen. Buy the Eggnog Ice Cream and assemble sundaes just before serving.

Chicken-Sausage Turnovers

Sauté 8 chicken thighs in ¼ cup cooking oil (use part butter if you wish) in a large frying pan. When browned on all sides, add ½ cup chicken stock made from chicken stock base. Cover and simmer until tender, about 20 minutes. Remove thighs; cool. Blend ¼ cup flour and ½ teaspoon salt into pan drippings; slowly stir in 2 cups milk. Cook over medium heat, stirring constantly until thickened; cool.

Meanwhile, cook 8 pork sausage links; drain. Remove bone from each chicken thigh, leaving the meat in one piece; place a cooked pork sausage in the opening. Make pastry based on 4 cups flour (or use 2 packages pie crust mix). Roll out pastry, cut into eight 7-inch rounds. Place a piece of chicken on each round; top with 2 tablespoons of the cooled gravy. Moisten pastry edges and fold to make turnover; seal edges. Place turnovers on a baking sheet; bake in a moderately hot oven (375°) for 30 minutes or until brown. Serve hot with reheated remaining gravy. Makes 8 servings.

Limas with Lemon-Dill Butter

Cook 3 packages (10 oz. each) frozen limas as directed on the package. Meanwhile melt 4 tablespoons butter in a saucepan; season with ½ teaspoon dill weed and 2 tablespoons lemon juice. When ready to serve, put drained limas in a large serving bowl, pour butter over, garnish with lemon slices and parsley. Makes 8 servings.

Avocado-Beet Salad

1 can (1 lb.) sliced beets
1 package unflavored gelatin
1 cup orange juice
2 tablespoons mayonnaise
¾ teaspoon salt
¼ teaspoon pepper
4 avocados, peeled and halved
  Juice of 1 lemon
  Lettuce leaves
  Mayonnaise dressing
  Parsley

Drain liquid from beets; put liquid in a small saucepan and bring to a boil. Soften gelatin in ½ cup of the orange juice; add the boiling beet liquid, stirring to dissolve gelatin. Put mixture in an electric blender, add beets, remaining orange juice, mayonnaise, salt, and pepper; whirl until smooth. Pour into a bowl and refrigerate until set, at least 2 hours. Shortly before serving time, prepare avocados and coat each with lemon juice. Place each half on a lettuce leaf and arrange on serving tray. Using a serving spoon, make large scoops from beet gelatin and place in the hollowed avocado centers. Place a bowl of mayonnaise in the center of the tray and garnish with parsley. Refrigerate until ready to serve. Makes 8 servings.

Eggnog Ice Cream

Scoop eggnog ice cream into sherbet glasses. Top with sweetened, rum-flavored whipped cream. Garnish with chocolate curls.

Menu

Spiced Chicken
Hot Brown Rice
Green Salad
Buttered Zucchini
Sourdough French Rolls with Butter
Fresh Plums with Light Cream

This menu is a good one for drop-in guests. It is based on a flavorful chicken dish that you can make even if the chicken is frozen. Use fresh zucchini and ready-made rolls.

If the chicken is frozen, start cooking it first. Then start the rice. Make the salad of mixed greens; dress it with your favorite dressing. Slice the zucchini and cook for 10 to 15 minutes in a small amount of water; season with butter, salt, and pepper. Buy the rolls from your grocery or bakery. For dessert, halve and pit fresh plums, sweeten, and serve with cream.

Spiced Chicken

1 broiler-fryer chicken (2½ to 3 pounds), cut up
2 cups orange juice
1 teaspoon salt
½ teaspoon nutmeg
1 teaspoon sweet basil
1 clove garlic, halved
1½ cups sliced fresh peaches
2 tablespoons flour
¼ teaspoon salt
  Dash of pepper

Put into pan the chicken, orange juice, 1 teaspoon salt, nutmeg, sweet basil, and garlic; simmer until chicken is tender (35 minutes; or 45 to 60 minutes if chicken is frozen). Remove chicken to a warm dish, and arrange on top the sliced peaches; keep hot. Strain stock, measure 1½ cups, and gradually stir this into flour, keeping the mixture smooth. Add the salt and pepper. Cook over medium heat, stirring until thickened. Pour over the chicken and peaches. Makes 4 servings.

Menu

Hot or Chilled Chicken Consommé

Cornish Game Hens

Mandarin Orange Dressing

Fluffy Cheese Rice

Buttered Fresh Asparagus

Crisp Green Salad

Cheesecake

This menu contains several shortcuts. Buy the chicken consommé, chill it in the can, and serve it jellied with a twist of lemon; or open and heat just before you plan to serve it. Make the green salad and crisp it in the refrigerator ahead; then add your favorite French dressing at the table.

Stuff the game hens ahead if you wish, but begin roasting them about 1 to 1¼ hours before serving time. While the hens are in the oven, prepare the rice and cook the asparagus; season the asparagus with butter, lemon juice, salt, and pepper. Buy a frozen cheesecake.

Cornish Game Hens with Mandarin Orange Dressing

2 cans (11 oz. each) mandarin oranges, drained, liquid reserved
1 small can (2 oz.) sliced pimiento
4 Cornish game hens
4 tablespoons soy sauce
4 tablespoons lemon or lime juice

Combine the orange sections with the pimiento. Use this mixture to stuff game hens lightly. Truss and place the birds in a baking pan. Roast in a moderate oven (350°) for 50 to 60 minutes or until the leg moves easily when jiggled. Baste while cooking with the reserved orange liquid combined with soy sauce and lemon or lime juice.

Fluffy Cheese Rice

1 cup uncooked rice
2½ cups chicken broth
1 tablespoon butter
1/16 teaspoon powdered saffron
¼ cup hot water
1 cup shredded Swiss cheese

Combine rice with chicken broth in a pan; add butter and bring to a boil. Cover, turn heat to lowest setting and cook for 20 minutes or until rice has absorbed the liquid. Combine saffron with hot water and stir to dissolve completely. Add to the rice after it has cooked 10 minutes. When the rice is cooked, fold in Swiss cheese. Do not stir or the cheese will get stringy. Serve the rice hot. Makes 4 servings.

Menu

Avocado Soup

Roasted Leg of Lamb

Armenian Pilaf

Eggplant Relish

Sliced Tomatoes

Orange Sherbet   Cookies

Cuisines of the Near East inspired the choice of flavors combined in this menu. A simple, delicious avocado soup introduces an equally simple and delicious roast leg of lamb with appropriate accompaniments. Everything except the lamb and the pilaf can be prepared in advance.

You can roast the leg of lamb in the oven or in a covered barbecue. If you wish, have your meatman bone and tie the leg so you can roast it on a spit.

Avocado Soup

2 tablespoons butter or margarine
2 tablespoons minced onion
1 large can (6 or 8 oz.) mushroom stems and
 pieces
2 tablespoons cornstarch
3 cups chicken broth (fresh, canned, or made
 with stock concentrate)
 Salt and pepper to taste
1 large avocado, peeled and diced

Melt butter or margarine in a saucepan. Add minced onion and cook until soft. Drain mushrooms, reserving liquid. Chop mushrooms; add to onions and cook another minute or two. Blend cornstarch with a little of the broth, then mix with remaining broth. Add to onions, along with the mushroom liquid; cook, stirring, until thickened.

Season the soup with salt and pepper. Just before serving, add avocado. (You can chill the soup base, then reheat and add the avocado just before serving.) Makes 6 servings.

Armenian Pilaf

6 tablespoons butter or margarine
1½ cups broken pieces vermicelli (or other thin
 noodles)
1 cup rice
½ teaspoon salt
2 cups boiling water

In a saucepan, melt butter or margarine; add vermicelli. Cook, stirring, until well browned. Add rice, salt, and boiling water; stir and cover. Boil slowly for 10 minutes. Remove from heat and let stand covered for 15 to 20 minutes. Keep warm in oven if not served immediately. Makes 6 servings.

Eggplant Relish

2 tablespoons butter or margarine
3 tablespoons salad oil
2 whole cloves garlic, peeled
1 large eggplant, cubed (unpeeled or peeled)
3 tablespoons chopped onion
½ teaspoon dried basil
1 teaspoon salt
½ cup yogurt
½ cup sour cream
½ cup yogurt or sour cream
 Juice of ½ lemon
 Lettuce
 Paprika
 Minced parsley

In a wide frying pan, heat butter or margarine and salad oil. Add garlic, eggplant, onion, basil, and salt. Cook over medium high heat, turning occasionally with a spatula, until eggplant is soft and lightly browned. Remove from heat and stir in ½ cup yogurt and ½ cup sour cream. Chill thoroughly. Mix with an additional ½ cup yogurt or sour cream and lemon juice. Spoon into a lettuce-lined bowl and sprinkle liberally with paprika and minced parsley. Makes 6 servings.

Menu

Lamb Chops Madeira
Oven Risotto with Peas
Spring Garden Relishes
Bananas in Cardamom Cream

You can rely on your oven to complete the cooking of thick, juicy chops and the rice casserole for this small dinner. Frozen peas in butter sauce, which you cook in the freezer wrap, are added at the last moment to the risotto.

Slim green onions, fancily-cut celery, and plump cherry tomatoes assume the dual role of salad and relish. Serve crusty rolls and sweet or regular butter.

Before you actually begin to cook dinner, have the relishes chilling, the table set, and the ingredients for the dessert together and measured. Start the lamb chops and when they are almost browned enough, start the rice. These two dishes should go

into the oven at the same time. While they bake, you can make the meat sauce and cook the peas for the rice. Sauté the bananas and glaze with cream just before serving.

Lamb Chops Madeira

4 lamb loin chops, each cut 2 inches thick
 Salt and pepper
2 tablespoons butter
¼ pound mushrooms, sliced
1 can (10½ oz.) condensed beef broth
⅓ cup Madeira or Port
2 tablespoons brandy or Cognac (optional)

Sprinkle chops lightly with salt and pepper. Melt butter in a wide frying pan and add chops, browning nicely on all sides. Remove to a pan and place in a moderately slow oven (325°) for 30 minutes. They will still be slightly pink inside. While chops are baking, discard all but 2 tablespoons of fat from browning pan; add the mushrooms to the remaining drippings and brown lightly. Pour in the beef broth and Madeira, and boil rapidly until reduced to about ¾ cup. Warm the brandy and pour, flaming, into the sauce. Keep the sauce warm or reheat to serve over the lamb chops. Add any juice from chops to sauce. Makes 4 servings.

This small company dinner of thick loin lamb chops demands little attention from the cook.

Oven Risotto with Peas

3 tablespoons butter
1 cup short-grain (pearl) rice
2 cups chicken broth (canned or freshly made)
1 package (10 oz.) peas frozen in butter sauce (in a pouch)
½ cup shredded Parmesan cheese
 Salt to taste
1 avocado, peeled, pitted, sliced

Melt butter in a pan you can put in the oven. Stir in rice and cook, stirring, until rice is lightly toasted. Add chicken broth and bring to a boil. Cover and bake in a moderately slow oven (325°)

for 30 minutes, or until liquid is absorbed and rice is tender. In the meantime, cook peas as directed on the carton. When rice is cooked, stir peas and sauce into it, along with Parmesan cheese. Add salt; garnish with avocado. Makes 4 to 6 servings.

Bananas in Cardamom Cream

Melt 4 tablespoons butter in a wide frying pan and stir in 2 tablespoons sugar and ⅛ teaspoon cardamom. Peel 4 medium-sized bananas and cut in slices about 1 inch thick. Add to pan and cook quickly over highest heat, shaking or turning with a spatula, until lightly brown on all sides. Squeeze juice of ½ lemon into pan and add ¼ cup heavy cream. Boil rapidly, stirring carefully so as not to mash bananas, until sauce thickens slightly. Serve the fruit hot, spooning into individual dessert dishes. Pour additional heavy cream over each portion if you like. Makes 4 servings.

Menu

Chilled Tomato Dill Soup

Beef Stroganoff

Buttered Baked Potato

Butter Lettuce and Romaine

with Onion Dressing

Sliced Fresh Pears with Cream

and Brown Sugar

This menu offers a new approach to beef stroganoff, for it is served over a baked, buttered potato. Start the meal with a chilled tomato soup made with fresh tomatoes.

Make the tomato soup ahead and chill. Wash, dry, and crisp the lettuce; make the dressing using onion-flavored salad dressing mix (follow directions on the package). Prepare the stroganoff ahead and keep warm or rewarm just before serving. Bake the potatoes and have your guests butter them at the table. Spoon the stroganoff over each individual portion. Serve fresh sliced pears for dessert with cream and brown sugar.

Chilled Tomato Dill Soup

Peel 4 medium-sized tomatoes; cut in quarters and whirl in a blender until smooth (or press through a wire strainer). Combine with 2 cups cold buttermilk, ¾ teaspoon salt, and ½ teaspoon dill weed. Mix well and chill at least 30 minutes. Makes 6 servings.

Beef Stroganoff

- 2 tablespoons flour
- 2 teaspoons salt
- ¼ teaspoon pepper
- 2 pounds top sirloin, cut in ¼-inch strips
- 4 tablespoons butter
- ½ cup finely chopped onion
- 1 clove garlic, minced
- 1 pound fresh mushrooms, sliced
- 1 cup sour cream
- ½ cup milk
    Chopped parsley
    Baked potatoes

Combine the flour, salt, and pepper, and dredge the meat in the mixture until all pieces are evenly coated. Melt the butter in a frying pan and add the onion, garlic, and meat; brown meat over medium to high heat, stirring constantly. Cover, lower heat to simmering, and cook 15 minutes. Remove meat; reserve. Add mushrooms to the pan, browning them in the pan drippings, turning frequently with a spatula; cook for 10 minutes. Return meat to pan and combine thoroughly. Cover and simmer until meat is tender, about 30 minutes. Just before serving, stir in the sour cream and milk; heat, but do not boil. Garnish with chopped parsley and serve over hot buttered baked potatoes. Makes 6 servings.

Menu

Sparkling Boysenberry Soup

Butter Lettuce Hearts with

Gorgonzola Dressing

Carpet Bag Steaks

Butter-Roasted Potato Balls

Fresh Green Beans

French Chocolate Cups

In New Zealand and Australia, the luxurious combination of beef tenderloin steak stuffed with oysters is prosaically named "carpet bags."

Berry soup, a favorite summer treat in northern Europe, is the sprightly beginning for this meal; serve it in the living room before dinner. You can make the soup, salad, and dessert well ahead of time, and complete the preparation of the meat and vegetables to the point of cooking. You might let the green beans finish cooking and the steaks broil while you are eating the salad. You can brown the potatoes before you sit down to dinner; keep them warm over very low heat.

Sparkling Boysenberry Soup

  4 cups boysenberries (or blackberries or
     loganberries), washed and drained
     About ½ cup sugar
 ½ cup water
  2 tablespoons cornstarch
  2 to 3-inch cinnamon stick
1½ tablespoons lemon juice
  1 bottle (7 oz.) chilled ginger ale
     Sour cream

Reserve 6 of the nicest berries and coarsely mash the remainder. Sweeten the fruit lightly with sugar. Add water. Dissolve cornstarch in a little of the juice and blend with berries; add cinnamon stick. Cook fruit, stirring, until thickened slightly and clear. Stir in lemon juice and chill. Remove cinnamon stick and mix in ginger ale. Ladle soup into pretty bowls. Spoon a generous dollop of sour cream into each bowl and top with a reserved berry. Makes 6 servings.

Butter Lettuce Hearts with Gorgonzola Dressing

Shake ⅔ cup olive oil or salad oil with ¼ cup lemon juice, ½ cup coarsely crumbled Gorgonzola cheese, ½ teaspoon salt, and ¼ teaspoon black pepper. Cover and let stand at room temperature for several hours. Break in bite-sized pieces enough choice leaves from the hearts of several heads of crisp, clean butter lettuce to make about 6 cups. Chill, covered, until ready to serve, then mix with the prepared dressing and spoon on chilled salad plates. Makes 6 servings.

Carpet Bag Steaks

  6 beef tenderloin fillet steaks, each cut
     1½ inches thick
 ⅔ to ¾ cup small oysters, fresh or canned
  1 tablespoon butter, cut in small pieces
  1 teaspoon salt
 ¼ teaspoon pepper
     Melted butter
     Salt and pepper

Make a pocket in each steak by cutting along one side and slipping the knife tip well into the center of the meat. Mix oysters with butter pieces, the 1 teaspoon salt, and ¼ teaspoon pepper. Stuff each steak with oysters; close the pocket with small skewers, lacing with string if necessary to hold shut. Brush steaks with melted butter and broil about 6 inches from heat source for 6 minutes on each side for rare, 8 minutes for medium, and 10

minutes or more for well done. Season to taste with salt and pepper. Makes 6 servings.

Butter-Roasted Potato Balls

Peel frying potatoes and shape 3 cups potato balls with the large end of a melon or French ball cutter. Cover potatoes with cold water until ready to cook; drain thoroughly. Melt 6 tablespoons butter in a wide frying pan. Add potatoes and cook, covered, over medium heat until potatoes are browned on all sides, 20 to 25 minutes. Shake occasionally to turn the potatoes. Add ½ cup finely chopped sweet onion, ¾ teaspoon salt, and a dash of coarsely ground black pepper; cook 10 minutes more, or until onion is soft. Keep warm over very low heat; pour over green beans (recipe follows) to serve. Makes 6 servings.

Fresh Green Beans

Remove tips and strings from 1½ pounds green beans. Cook, covered, in ½ cup boiling water with 1 teaspoon salt for 12 to 15 minutes, or until tender. Drain and serve with potato balls.

French Chocolate Cups

  1 cup semi-sweet chocolate pieces
  2 egg yolks
  ¼ cup warm water
  1 cup heavy cream
  ¼ cup powdered sugar
  ½ teaspoon ground cinnamon
     Whole blanched almonds (optional)

Stir chocolate pieces over hot water until melted. Beat egg yolks with warm water; blend into chocolate. Remove from heat and chill for about 10 minutes. Meanwhile, whip the cream with the powdered sugar and cinnamon. Fold cream into chocolate mixture and spoon into 6 individual chocolate cups or small dessert bowls. Chill until ready to serve. Garnish with almonds, if you wish. Makes 6 servings.

Menu

Hearts of Palm Green Salad
Lobster Tails or Salmon Steaks
with Macadamia Butter
Steamed Rice with Cherry Tomatoes
Hot Italian Green Beans
Croissants
Hot Banana Sundaes

This festive company dinner can be prepared in half an hour, once you complete the shopping. It's an excellent menu to serve unexpected guests.

Hearts of Palm Green Salad

Garnish your favorite mixed green salad with sliced canned hearts of palm, sliced hard-cooked egg, and crumbled Roquefort cheese.

Lobster Tails or Salmon Steaks with Macadamia Butter

Have your fish market split 4 lobster tails (8 oz. each) in half, lengthwise through the center. (Or, if you are using prepackaged frozen lobster tails, let them thaw slightly, then cut in half lengthwise with a very sharp knife.) Drop lobster tails into boiling salted water and simmer gently for 6 minutes. Drain. Arrange tails on a baking sheet and brush with 2 tablespoons melted butter. Place under the broiler about 4 inches and broil just until lightly browned, about 4 to 5 minutes. Heat ¼ cup butter until it just starts to brown, add ¼ cup chopped macadamia nuts, and heat just for a minute. Spoon nut sauce over lobster. Makes 4 servings.

You can substitute salmon steaks for lobster

tails. Broil the fish steaks, brushed with butter, on both sides before topping with hot nut butter.

Steamed Rice with Cherry Tomatoes

Prepare a packaged herb-seasoned rice as directed on the package. Add a few halved cherry tomatoes the last few minutes of cooking.

Hot Banana Sundaes

Melt 2 tablespoons butter in a chafing dish or frying pan. Add ¼ cup sugar, ¼ cup orange juice, and the grated peel of 1 orange. Let simmer a few minutes, until thickened. Add 4 bananas, peeled and sliced diagonally, and heat. If you wish, flame with 2 tablespoons warm rum. Spoon over scoops of vanilla ice cream and sprinkle with grated chocolate. Makes 4 servings.

Menu

Parmesan Breaded Veal

Asparagus and Peas Italian

Wild Rice Pilaf

Green Salad   Hot Rolls

Lemon Pie

None of the dishes for this meal is difficult, but except for the dessert, each requires a bit of attention shortly before serving. The entire meal is particularly suited to service on a cart fitted with a warming tray on top.

Make or buy the Lemon Pie. Organize the utensils and ingredients for the last-minute cooking of the breaded cutlets, rice, and vegetables. Shortly before you begin the final cooking, prepare the salad greens, which you'll dress with oil and vinegar or your favorite dressing just before serving. Heat rolls.

Parmesan Breaded Veal

1½ pounds veal cutlets, in ¼-inch slices
1½ teaspoons salt
¼   teaspoon white pepper
1½ teaspoons crumbled basil leaves
3   tablespoons grated Parmesan cheese
1   cup fine, dry bread crumbs
2   eggs, slightly beaten
⅓   cup olive oil or salad oil
    Lemon slices

Season meat with the salt, pepper, and basil. Dip into a mixture of the Parmesan and bread crumbs, then into eggs, again into crumbs; chill ½ hour or more. Heat oil in a heavy frying pan and brown the veal quickly on both sides. Reduce heat; continue cooking, uncovered, for about 15 minutes. Serve hot, topped with fresh lemon slices. Makes 4 servings.

Asparagus and Peas Italian

½   cup water
¾   teaspoon salt
3   tablespoons olive oil or butter
1   tablespoon freshly chopped parsley
    Dash of pepper
1   package (9 oz.) frozen asparagus tips
2   packages (10 oz. each) frozen peas

Bring water to a boil in a large saucepan; add salt, olive oil, parsley, pepper, asparagus, and peas. When it returns to a boil, reduce heat; cook, covered, for about 5 minutes, then remove lid and cook 2 to 3 minutes longer. Drain and serve immediately. Makes 4 to 6 servings.

Menu

Florentined Sole
Parsley Potato Balls
Cucumber Salad
Hot Cheese Rolls
Raspberry Mousse with Peaches

This menu makes use of several shortcuts, with very good results. Assemble the fish entrée, fruit dessert, and a favorite marinated cucumber salad several hours before guests arrive. Heat frozen shredded potato balls on top of the range or in the oven, whichever suits you and your kitchen, and sprinkle liberally with minced parsley before serving. You can bake the rolls along with the fish.

Florentined Sole

3 packages (10 oz. each) frozen chopped
  spinach
2 cups (1 pt.) sour cream
3 tablespoons flour
½ cup finely chopped green onions, including
  some of the tops
  Juice of 1 lemon
2 teaspoons salt
1½ to 2 pounds thin fillets of sole
2 tablespoons butter or margarine
  Paprika

Cook spinach according to directions on the box. Drain very thoroughly. Blend sour cream with flour, onions, lemon juice, and salt. Combine half this mixture with spinach. Spread spinach evenly over bottom of a shallow baking dish, about 10 by 15 inches (choose one suitable for serving). Arrange sole fillets on spinach, overlapping as needed. Dot with butter or margarine. Spread remaining sour cream evenly over sole, leaving a border to show spinach if you like. Dust lightly with paprika. (At this point you can refrigerate the dish until ready to cook.) Bake in a moderately hot oven (375°) for 25 minutes, or until fish flakes when broken with a fork. Makes 6 to 8 servings.

Hot Cheese Rolls

Generously sprinkle refrigerated crescent rolls with grated American or Romano cheese before shaping. Form into crescents as directed on package and place on greased baking sheet. Bake in a moderately hot oven (375°) for 10 to 13 minutes.

Raspberry Mousse with Peaches

1 package (4¾ oz.) raspberry-currant flavored
  pudding mix
1 cup water
¼ teaspoon grated lemon peel
  Juice of 1 lemon
1 package (10 oz.) frozen raspberries, thawed
  (or 1½ cups fresh raspberries and 2
  tablespoons sugar)
1 cup (½ pt.) heavy cream
  Sliced peaches, fresh, frozen, or canned

In a saucepan, blend raspberry-currant pudding mix with water, lemon peel, lemon juice, and raspberries. Bring to a boil and cook, stirring, for 1 or 2 minutes. Chill. Whip the cream and fold into the raspberry mixture. Spoon into a serving bowl and chill. Decorate just before serving with peaches. Pass more peaches to spoon over individual desserts. Makes 6 servings.

Spicy lamb "sosaties" (South African kebabs) are served with hot fruit, rice, mixed green salad for outdoor barbecue dinner. Menu and recipes are on pages 88 and 89.

Barbecues and Picnics

Outdoor meals offer endless opportunity for quick and easy dinners and really do give the cook time to relax. They may range from tail-gate picnics, bicycle outings, and camp cooking, to patio and barbecue meals. The food may be carried ready to eat to the chosen site, or cooked after you get there. And whether you take to the open road or eat in your own back yard, this chapter contains menus for all sorts of occasions.

The whole family can help prepare many of the barbecue meals, some of which make good holiday food. Others, with gourmet appeal, lend themselves as guest dinners. Should a time arise when you need to serve a number of children at a barbecue, you'll even find a barbecue menu designed to please youngsters. If the weather disappoints you, most of the menus are easily adapted to indoor cooking.

Menu

Chopped Liver with Toast
Anchovy Grilled Steak
Three-Bean Salad
Sliced Tomatoes
Peach Flambé or Fresh Peach Sundae

This dinner, which will appeal to epicures, may be prepared ahead of time except for the grilling of the steak and the flaming of the dessert. If charcoal cookery is the man's job in the family, there will be little last-minute work for the hostess.

Chopped Liver with Toast

Bake a 2-pound chunk of calf or baby beef liver, unseasoned, in a moderate oven (350°) until an inserted meat thermometer reaches 150° (meat is still pink and juicy). Remove the skin and any veins and chop it with a French knife in very small cubes. (Do not grind.) Now chop 1 bunch green onions and cook in ¼ cup rendered chicken fat (or butter) until wilted. Add to the liver, along with any juices, and chill. Just before serving, stir in another ¼ cup chicken fat and salt to taste. (Do not add salt until the last minute; it will spoil the flavor.) Serve on lettuce leaves, accompanied by hot buttered rye toast. The toast may be made over the coals in the barbecue or in an electric toaster on the patio. Makes 12 servings.

Anchovy Grilled Steak

The steak may be any cut you wish. If you buy two 2-inch-thick boneless sirloins to serve 12, you can slice the steak in portions to suit all appetites. Make the marinade by chopping 2 small cans (2 oz. each) anchovy fillets and mixing them, oil and all, with 1 cup olive oil, ½ cup chopped parsley, 2 crushed cloves garlic, and a plentiful amount of coarsely ground black pepper. Let the steaks stand in this for 2 or 3 hours, turning them at least once. Heat the remaining marinade to be used as a sauce after the steaks are grilled to the desired doneness.

Three-Bean Salad

1 can (1 lb.) cut green beans
1 can (1 lb.) cut yellow wax beans
1 can (1 lb.) red kidney beans
1 small green pepper, finely chopped
1 small onion, finely chopped
¾ cup sugar
1 teaspoon salt
½ teaspoon freshly ground pepper
½ cup each vinegar and salad oil

Drain the liquid from the green beans, wax beans, and kidney beans. Place beans in a glass bowl and mix in green pepper and onion. Combine sugar, salt, pepper, vinegar, and oil; pour over bean mixture and mix well. Refrigerate until ready to serve. This is best if mixed the day before using so the vegetables will be well marinated.

Peach Flambé

Peel 12 whole ripe peaches very carefully, then roll each one in raspberry jam that has been forced through a strainer. Mix together equal parts grated almonds and sugar, and roll peaches in this mixture until well coated. Arrange in a large shallow heatproof bowl, but do not chill. Just before serving, heat ½ cup Jamaica rum and pour over the fruit. Light and serve when the flames have died down. Ice cream may also be served.

Menu

Barbecued Cross-Rib Roast
Curried New Potatoes, Green Onions
Mixed Greens Salad
Oil and Vinegar Dressing
Corn Bread Sticks
Ice Cream Pie
Strawberry-Blueberry Sauce

This meal is not elaborate, but the foods and flavors are exceptionally compatible and appropriate for family and friends. The menu is for eight.

You can do much of the preparation ahead. Dessert comes from the freezer and may be made days in advance: Pack a graham cracker crust or regular baked pie crust with vanilla ice cream (an 8 or 9-inch pan holds 1 to 1½ quarts ice cream and serves 6 to 8); wrap airtight and freeze. Let pie stand about 30 minutes in the refrigerator before cutting to serve.

Cornbread sticks, made from a mix or your own recipe, can also be baked ahead and frozen, then reheated in the oven.

The roast marinates overnight, and the new potatoes can be boiled the day before. Sauté the potatoes in butter with onions and seasonings while the roast browns. The fruit sauce for the pie is served cold, so prepare it early in the day.

Let salad greens crisp overnight, then mix with a favorite oil and vinegar dressing.

Barbecued Cross-Rib Roast

4 to 5-pound boneless, tied, beef cross-rib roast
⅓ cup catsup
¾ cup dry red wine (or ½ cup water and ¼ cup red wine vinegar)
½ cup salad oil
1 tablespoon instant minced onion
1 tablespoon Worcestershire
1 teaspoon crumbled rosemary
1½ teaspoons salt
¼ teaspoon monosodium glutamate
¼ teaspoon pepper
5 drops liquid smoke seasoning (optional)

Set the roast in a deep, close fitting bowl. Blend together the catsup, dry red wine, salad oil, instant minced onion, Worcestershire, rosemary, salt, monosodium glutamate, pepper, and liquid smoke seasoning, if desired. Pour this mixture over the roast; if it does not cover the meat, turn the roast several times while marinating. Cover and refrigerate 12 to 24 hours. Lift meat from marinade and insert a meat thermometer into the center. Cook the roast on a rotisserie, in a covered barbecue, or in the oven, basting frequently with marinade. On a rotisserie, place meat 6 inches above medium-hot coals. In a covered barbecue, have medium coals. In the oven, set the temperature at moderately slow (325°). All methods of cooking require about 1½ hours for rare to medium-rare meat. The meat thermometer should register 130° for rare or 140° for medium-rare to medium. (This is lower than typical for beef, but because the cross-rib is so lean, the outer edge of the roast would be overcooked if you allow it to reach standard temperature register.) Let roast stand about 20 minutes, then slice thinly and serve with meat juices. Makes 8 to 10 generous servings.

Curried New Potatoes and Green Onions

3 pounds small new potatoes, scrubbed,
  but not peeled
  Boiling water
  About 1 cup (½ lb.) butter or margarine
2 teaspoons curry powder
2 teaspoons mustard seed
2 cups (about 2 bunches) chopped green onions,
  including tops

Drop potatoes into enough boiling water to cover. Cover pan and simmer for 20 to 30 minutes or until potatoes are tender when pierced. Drain and let cool (overnight if desired). Coarsely chop unpeeled potatoes. Melt ½ cup of the butter or margarine in a wide frying pan over high heat. Add potatoes and cook, stirring with a spatula frequently, for about 5 minutes. Add more butter as needed (as much as an additional ½ cup). Sprinkle curry powder and mustard seed over potatoes and stir in well. Continue to cook, stirring frequently, until some of the potatoes are lightly browned. Mix in green onions. Cook until heated; salt to taste and serve. Makes 8 servings.

Strawberry-Blueberry Sauce

 ½ cup water
 ¾ cup sugar
 1 cup blueberries, fresh or unsweetened frozen
1½ tablespoons cornstarch
1½ tablespoons water
 1 tablespoon lemon juice
 ½ teaspoon vanilla
 2 cups whole medium-sized strawberries,
   cleaned and hulled

In a small pan, heat water and sugar to boiling. Add blueberries and bring to a boil; simmer about 2 minutes. Skim fruit from liquid with a slotted spoon and set aside. Blend cornstarch and water to make a smooth paste, then stir into the blueberry liquid. Cook, stirring, until thickened, clear and bubbling vigorously. Remove from heat and add lemon juice and vanilla. Let cool slightly and return blueberries to sauce. Chill, covered. Gently mix in strawberries. Keep cold, covered, until ready to spoon over wedges of ice cream pie. Makes enough for 8 servings.

Menu

Lemon-Lime Tomato Juice

Assorted Crisp Vegetables

Barbecued Steak with Garlic Baste

Chilled Whole Cauliflower with

Guacamole on Lettuce

Hot Buttered Green Beans

French Bread

Melon Compote   Mint Whipped Cream

Serve this meal indoors or out, but in either case, cook the steak outdoors while your guests sip the tangy Lemon-Lime Tomato Juice and munch crisp vegetables. The menu is designed to serve six.

The ingredients for the tomato juice cocktail should chill several hours before time to serve. Prepare the crisp vegetables of your choice — carrot curls, turnip sticks, raw asparagus tips, green onions — and chill until serving time. Cook the cauliflower several hours ahead and chill; mask it with guacamole just before serving.

Prepare the melon compote; mix and chill. To serve, arrange it over ice in a bowl and have it on the table when you serve the main course. Serve the mint-flavored whipped cream in a small bowl. Cook the beans at the last minute and season with butter, salt, and pepper. Serve them in a warmed casserole with a cover if the meal is eaten outdoors.

Lemon-Lime Tomato Juice

¼ cup lemon juice
¼ cup lime juice
1 tray ice cubes
1 large can (1 qt.) tomato juice, chilled
2 cans (12 oz. each) chilled lemon-lime flavored soda
Thin slices of lime

Combine lemon juice and lime juice in a large pitcher or bowl. Just before serving, add ice cubes to the mixture. Then pour in chilled tomato juice and chilled lemon-lime flavored soda. Garnish with lime slices. Makes about 10 cups.

Barbecued Steak with Garlic Baste

3½-pound top sirloin or top round steak
1 clove garlic, crushed
2 tablespoons finely chopped parsley
1 teaspoon salt
½ teaspoon pepper
2 tablespoons salad oil or olive oil
Unseasoned powdered meat tenderizer (optional)

Rub both sides of the steak with a mixture of crushed garlic, chopped parsley, salt, pepper, and salad oil or olive oil. Let steak stand 1 to 2 hours before barbecuing. If you wish to tenderize round steak, omit salt from baste and treat the steak one half hour before barbecuing with meat tenderizer as directed on the package. Cook the steak over hot coals until done to your liking, turning once to brown both sides well. Slice thinly to serve. Makes 6 servings.

Chilled Whole Cauliflower with Guacamole on Lettuce

1 medium-sized cauliflower
Salted water
2 tablespoons salad oil
Salt and pepper to taste
1 avocado, mashed (about 1 cup)
4 tablespoons lemon juice
4 tablespoons minced canned California green chilies
4 tablespoons chopped green onion
¾ teaspoon salt
¼ cup sour cream
Dash liquid hot-pepper seasoning
Crisp romaine lettuce
Radish roses for garnish

Cook cauliflower in salted water until tender crisp when tested with a fork (10 to 15 minutes). Drain, sprinkle with salad oil and salt and pepper to taste; chill. Combine mashed avocado with lemon juice, chilies, green onion, salt, sour cream, and liquid hot-pepper seasoning. Whirl in a blender until smooth. Just before serving, put cauliflower on a large platter and surround with crisp romaine lettuce. Cover with the avocado mixture and garnish with radish roses. Makes 6 to 8 servings.

This steak barbecue is simple enough to be served indoors or out, depending on the weather.

Menu

Top-of-Stove Macaroni and Cheese,
De Luxe
Dill Pickles, Cherry Tomatoes
Italian Bread Sticks
Red Apples
Mint Molasses Cookies
Hot Coffee or Hot Chocolate

A one-dish meal to reheat over a small camp stove is the mainstay of this picnic. The quickest way to heat the dish is on a portable camp or picnic stove.

Top-of-Stove Macaroni and Cheese, De Luxe

1 package (8 oz.) macaroni
  Boiling salted water
1 cup chopped green pepper
¼ cup chopped onion
½ cup chopped celery
¼ cup (⅛ lb.) butter or margarine
1 can (10½ oz.) white sauce
2 cups shredded process American cheese (about ½ lb.)
1 can (3 or 4 oz.) whole mushrooms
1 teaspoon salt
1 teaspoon prepared mustard
1 teaspoon Worcestershire
1 cup fine dry bread crumbs
2 tablespoons butter
½ teaspoon thyme
½ teaspoon oregano
½ cup milk

Cook macaroni in boiling salted water until just tender; drain and rinse. Cook green pepper, onion, and celery in the ¼ cup butter until soft. Add white sauce, cheese, and mushrooms (including mushroom liquid); cook, stirring constantly, until cheese melts. Add salt, mustard, and Worcestershire. In a heavy kettle first put the cooked macaroni, pour over the cheese sauce. Cook over low heat for 20 minutes, stirring gently from time to time to keep it from sticking. Meanwhile, brown crumbs in the 2 tablespoons butter; add thyme and oregano; pack in a separate container to take to the picnic.

To reheat the macaroni dish at the picnic, add the ½ cup milk; cook over low heat for 20 minutes. Sprinkle with the crumb mixture; serve. Makes 6 servings.

Mint Molasses Cookies

2 cups all-purpose flour (sift before measuring)
¼ teaspoon salt
2 teaspoons soda
1 teaspoon ginger
1 teaspoon cinnamon
½ teaspoon ground cloves
¾ cup shortening
1 cup brown sugar, firmly packed
¼ teaspoon mint extract
1 egg
¼ cup molasses
¼ cup granulated sugar

Sift flour again with the salt, soda, and spices. Thoroughly cream together the shortening, brown sugar, and mint extract. Beat in the egg until light and fluffy. Add molasses; mix well. Mix in dry ingredients until well blended. Chill at least 2 hours. Shape in balls the size of walnuts. Roll in granulated sugar, and place 2 inches apart on a greased cooky sheet. Bake in a moderate oven (350°) until crisp and browned, about 15 minutes. Makes about 4 dozen cookies.

Menu

Foil-Wrapped Meatball Stew
Tomato Wedges
Buttered Buffet Rye Bread
Sliced Chilled Watermelon
Sliced Fresh Peaches
Chocolate Cookies

The occasion may arise when you need to make special provisions for children at a barbecue. Here is a menu based on individual meatball stews designed to please young palates. While the foil-wrapped stews cook on the coals, you'll be able to prepare the other simple items on the menu. The cookies might be ones you have made or bought.

Foil-Wrapped Meatball Stew

1 pound lean ground beef
1 can (4½ oz.) deviled ham
½ teaspoon salt
1 can (14½ oz.) potatoes, drained
1 can (8 oz.) onions, drained
1 package (10 oz.) frozen mixed vegetables
   Salt and pepper to taste
   About ¾ cup canned condensed tomato,
   Cheddar cheese, or mushroom soup, or
   catsup or tomato sauce

Blend ground beef with deviled ham and salt. Shape meat mixture in small balls, using about 1 tablespoon for each. Divide equally onto four 14-inch squares of double thickness of heavy duty foil. Add potatoes, onions, and frozen mixed vegetables, dividing among the four servings. Sprinkle with salt and pepper. Spoon on canned condensed tomato, Cheddar cheese, or mushroom soup, catsup, or tomato sauce, using about 3 tablespoons for each. Fold foil securely in center and at ends

to enclose the filling. Place on hot coals for about 20 minutes. Remove to plates, open carefully, and let steam escape. Eat directly from the foil. Makes 4 servings.

Menu

Lamb Sosaties with Fruit
Steamed Rice
Mixed Green Salad   French Dressing
Crisp Bread Sticks
Plum Spice Cake Roll

The method of cooking lamb kebabs called sosaties (pronounced so-sah-tees) comes from South Africa, reportedly brought there by Malayan slaves in the seventeenth century. Today sosaties, thin wooden skewers strung with small cubes of broiled marinated lamb, are popular as an entrée or snack. Since the meat is somewhat pepper-hot with sweet-sour overtones, milder flavored foods complete this menu. For dessert, sliced fresh plums in a cake roll are served with a tart cream cheese-cottage cheese filling.

Your preparations for this meal start the day before when you combine the ingredients for the marinade. Let the meat marinate overnight. Early in the second day, prepare and chill the dessert and the salad ingredients. While the barbecue coals are heating, string the meat on skewers. Steam the rice and make the salad while the meat cooks.

Lamb Sosaties with Fruit

1½ cups cider vinegar
3 tablespoons apricot or pineapple jam
1½ tablespoons curry powder
1½ tablespoons salt
1½ tablespoons brown sugar, firmly packed
¼ teaspoon pepper
4 small dried hot chili peppers, crushed (use only 1 or 2 for a milder marinade)
2 medium-sized onions, sliced
3 cloves garlic, mashed
6 fresh lemon or orange leaves or 2 dried bay leaves
4 pounds lean boneless lamb, cubed
About 6 cups fruit: pitted apricots, pineapple chunks, cantaloupe wedges, and spiced crabapples

In a pan, combine the vinegar, jam, curry, powder, salt, brown sugar, pepper, chili peppers, onions, garlic, and lemon, orange, or bay leaves. Bring to a boil to blend the flavors and cool. Pour the marinade over the meat; cover and refrigerate 8 to 10 hours or overnight. Just before you are ready to barbecue the meat, remove the pieces from the marinade and string on skewers. Place the meat over medium-hot coals; grill, turning to brown all sides, a total of 15 to 20 minutes.

Strain the marinade, discarding the onions and leaves; bring liquid to a boil and simmer about 5 minutes to concentrate it. Baste the meat occasionally with the marinade. String the fruit on skewers and lay on top of the meat during the last 5 to 10 minutes cooking time. Baste the fruit and the meat with the marinade. The fruit will also help baste the meat and should be on the grill long enough to be thoroughly heated but not soft. Makes about 8 servings.

Plum Spice Cake Roll

½ cup unsifted regular all-purpose flour
½ teaspoon baking powder
¼ teaspoon salt
⅛ teaspoon cinnamon
⅛ teaspoon nutmeg
⅛ teaspoon allspice
¼ teaspoon cream of tartar
4 eggs, separated
¾ cup sugar
½ teaspoon vanilla
1 cup sieved cottage cheese
4 ounces cream cheese
¼ cup sifted powdered sugar
1 tablespoon lemon juice
½ teaspoon grated lemon peel
2 cups thinly sliced firm ripe fresh plums
Sifted powdered sugar and sprigs of mint for garnish

Line a shallow baking pan (10 by 15 by 1 inch) with waxed paper. Sift flour together with the baking powder, salt, cinnamon, nutmeg, and allspice. Add the cream of tartar to the egg whites and beat until soft peaks form. Gradually add the sugar, beating until whites are smooth and glossy. Beat the yolks with the vanilla; gently fold into the whites along with the flour mixture. Spoon batter into the paper-lined pan and bake in a moderately hot oven (375°) for 12 to 15 minutes, or until cake springs back when lightly pressed. Loosen cake from sides of pan and turn out on a clean towel that has been dusted with powdered sugar. Peel off waxed paper and trim off crisp edges of cake. Starting with the narrow end of the cake, roll towel and cake together; cool on a rack. To make the filling, beat together the cottage cheese, cream cheese, sugar, lemon juice, and lemon peel. When the cake is cool, carefully unroll it, removing the towel. Spread the filling over the cake and arrange the sliced plums over the filling. (Reserve several plum slices for garnish.) Roll the cake and dust the top with sifted powdered sugar. Place on a serving platter and garnish with the reserved plum slices and sprigs of mint. Chill several hours before serving. Makes about 8 servings.

Menu

Spareribs Cantonese
Zucchini-Tomato Parmesan
Orange-Wheat Salad
Angel Food Cake   Cream and Berries

Spareribs Cantonese and Zucchini-Tomato Parmesan, assembled at home, cook on fire pit at picnic site.

This menu is as easily prepared over the campfire or barbecue grill as on the range. Start food preparation the evening before. Make the cake from a mix. Marinate the spareribs overnight. In the morning make the salad, reserving the orange sections, which should be mixed in just before serving. If you make this a picnic meal, take the whipping cream (or ready-to-serve whipped cream in an aerosol can) and the berries in a cooler. You can cook or partially cook both the spareribs and zucchini dishes, chill, and take them to the picnic site to finish cooking or to reheat.

Spareribs Cantonese

About 4 pounds country-style spareribs, cut in serving pieces
¾ cup soy sauce
¼ cup water
 1 cup orange marmalade
½ teaspoon garlic powder
¼ teaspoon pepper

Place spareribs in a large, shallow pan. Blend soy sauce with water, orange marmalade, garlic powder, and pepper. Pour over the spareribs. Marinate overnight, turning ribs once or twice. To cook, place spareribs in a heavy roasting pan or Dutch oven. Pour marinade over meat, then cover and place over a medium heat for 1 hour or longer. Baste occasionally with the marinade. Serve hot. Makes 4 to 6 servings.

Zucchini-Tomato Parmesan

 6 medium-sized zucchini squash, cut in ¼-inch rounds
 1 stalk celery, thinly sliced
 1 small onion, thinly sliced
 1 tablespoon Italian seasoning, or 1 teaspoon oregano and 1 teaspoon marjoram
 1 teaspoon salt
¼ teaspoon pepper
 1 can (8 oz.) tomato sauce
 3 medium-sized tomatoes, cut in ½-inch slices
¼ cup grated Parmesan cheese
 2 tablespoons butter

Arrange zucchini rounds in bottom of a buttered, large, shallow saucepan or frying pan. Add layers of the celery and onion. Sprinkle with Italian seasoning, salt, and pepper; pour over the tomato sauce. Arrange tomato slices on top, sprinkle with Parmesan, and dot with butter. Cover tightly and place over medium heat (on top of the range, the barbecue, or coals) for 35 to 45 minutes or until the zucchini is tender. Makes 6 servings.

Orange-Wheat Salad

1 cup quick-cooking cracked wheat or bulgur
2 tablespoons butter
2 cups water
¼ cup mayonnaise
   Juice of 1 lemon
   Juice of 1 orange
2 teaspoons chopped chives
1 teaspoon sugar
1 teaspoon salt
1 can (11 oz.) mandarin oranges, drained

Brown quick-cooking wheat in the butter in a large saucepan. Add 2 cups water, bring to a boil, cover, and simmer 15 minutes. Remove from heat, take off lid to let steam escape so the cooked wheat will dry a bit. When cracked wheat is cool, mix lightly to prevent kernels from sticking together and place in refrigerator until ready to add dressing. Make dressing by mixing together the mayonnaise, lemon juice, orange juice, chives, sugar, and salt. Mix with chilled wheat and orange sections. You might wish to save a few orange sections for garnish. Makes 4 to 6 servings.

Hearty whole meal sandwiches are ready to eat when the foil pie plate packages are opened.

Menu

Colossal Cartwheel Sandwiches
Baked Beans or Cole Slaw
Olives
Fig Bars
Bananas
Soft Drinks

This easy picnic menu features full-meal sandwiches. Each of the over-sized, open-plate sandwiches is carried on a paper plate with another plate inverted over the top. Individual servings of cole slaw can be taken in covered paper cups.

Colossal Cartwheel Sandwiches

1   round loaf French or rye bread, unsliced
½   cup (¼ lb.) softened butter or margarine
1   small package (3 oz.) cream cheese, softened
1   cup shredded sharp Cheddar cheese
1   teaspoon grated onion
¼   pound bologna
¼   pound salami
¼   pound pressed ham slices
½   pound Swiss cheese slices
    Hard-cooked egg slices
½   cup pickle relish
½   cup shredded corned beef
    Tomato wedges, radish slices

Remove the top and bottom crusts from the bread. Cut across the loaf to make 4 to 6 whole round slices. Blend well together the butter, cream cheese, Cheddar cheese, and onion until a smooth spreading consistency. Spread over each slice of bread. Arrange in pie-shaped sections on each slice a selection of meats, Swiss cheese, and egg slices. Pile pickle relish and shredded corned beef in the center; garnish with tomato and radish slices. Put each sandwich in a foil pie plate or paper plate. Cut sandwich in wedges and tie another plate over top. Makes 4 to 6 sandwiches.

Menu

Rosemary Barbecued Chicken
Lime Limas
Tropical Cabbage Salad
Walnut Torte

All members of the family can help prepare this meal if they are so inclined. Dad can tend the barbecue while he supervises a young son or daughter who has the fun of basting the chicken halves. The easy walnut dessert might be proudly served by the junior cook who baked it earlier in the day. Make the salad and specially flavored limas just before serving. If there's any extra herb sauce after the barbecue, refrigerate it for future use.

Rosemary Barbecued Chicken

2 broiler-fryer chickens (about 2 lbs. each), cut in half
½ cup olive oil or other salad oil
½ cup melted butter
½ cup white wine, or ½ cup water and 2 tablespoons lemon juice
1 teaspoon salt
¼ teaspoon freshly ground pepper
1 teaspoon crushed rosemary
1 clove garlic, minced or mashed

Brush chicken halves inside and out with a bubbling hot mixture of the olive oil or other salad oil, melted butter, white wine, salt, freshly ground pepper, crushed rosemary, and garlic. Place chicken halves, cavity side down, on grill about 4 inches above hot coals. Baste frequently and turn chicken about every 10 minutes. Total cooking time is 45 to 60 minutes. Makes 4 servings.

Lime Limas

Cook 2 packages (10 oz. each) frozen baby limas according to direction on packages. Drain, if needed. Stir in 1 tablespoon butter and 2 tablespoons thawed frozen limeade concentrate. Makes 6 servings.

Tropical Cabbage Salad

1 cup flaked coconut
1 medium-sized head cabbage, finely shredded
¾ cup sour cream
2½ tablespoons vinegar
¾ teaspoon salt
¼ teaspoon pepper
1 tablespoon sugar
Paprika
Toasted coconut

Add the flaked coconut to the shredded cabbage. Blend together the sour cream, vinegar, salt, pepper, and sugar. Mix lightly with cabbage and coconut. Sprinkle with paprika and toasted coconut. To toast coconut, spread a thin layer on a baking sheet and toast in a moderate oven (350°) until lightly browned, watching carefully and stirring when necessary; takes 3 or 4 minutes. Makes 6 to 8 servings.

Walnut Torte

3 eggs
1 cup sugar
1 cup crushed graham cracker crumbs
½ cup chopped walnuts
Currant jelly
Whipped cream

Beat eggs until thick and lemon colored. Add sugar, crumbs, and nut meats; mix well. Pour batter into a greased and floured 9-inch cake pan. Bake in a moderate oven (350°) for 25 minutes, or until torte tests done when you insert a cake tester. Cool in pan. Turn onto serving dish and spread top with layer of jelly; top with whipped cream. Cut in wedges. Makes 6 or 8 servings.

Menu

Barbecued Swordfish with Capers
Grilled Eggplant
Green Pea Salad
Sour Cream Dressing
Sourdough French Bread
Fresh Fruit Compote

꧁ᜟ꧂꧁ᜟ꧂꧁ᜟ꧂꧁ᜟ꧂꧁ᜟ꧂꧁ᜟ꧂꧁ᜟ꧂

An auxiliary barbecue might come in handy for the preparation of this meal, but you can get along with one large barbecue. Several hours before serving time, make a fruit compote and refrigerate it. Shortly before serving, prepare the baste for the swordfish and eggplant and make the salad. Heat the bread while the fish and eggplant are being grilled.

Barbecued Swordfish with Capers

  8 swordfish steaks, ¾ inch thick
     Lemon-butter baste (recipe below)
1½ tablespoons thinly sliced green onion tops
  1 tablespoon capers

Brush both sides of the swordfish steaks with the lemon-butter baste (recipe follows). Cook about 8 inches above medium-hot coals for about 7 minutes per side, basting once during cooking. Remove to a warm platter, sprinkle with the green onion and capers, and pour remaining lemon-butter over top. Makes 8 servings.

Lemon-Butter Baste:

In a small frying pan, heat ¾ cup (⅜ lb.) butter, the juice of one lemon, and ½ teaspoon salt. Use as a baste for swordfish (and the eggplant in the recipe to follow). Makes about 1 cup.

Grilled Eggplant

Wash and remove stems from 2 large eggplants; cut each in 8 wedges. Brush cut edges with lemon-butter baste (recipe above) and place with the skin side down on the barbecue grill, 6 to 8 inches above medium-hot coals for about 7 minutes. Then turn and cook on both cut sides about 4 minutes each, or until a dark brown crust forms. Serve immediately directly from the grill. Makes 8 servings of 2 wedges each.

Green Pea Salad
Sour Cream Dressing

  2 large packages (1 lb. 8 oz. each) frozen
     green peas
  4 green onion bulbs, thinly sliced
¾ cup sour cream
¾ teaspoon salt
¼ teaspoon pepper, preferably coarse ground
     Cucumber slices for garnish

Defrost peas (do not cook). Combine peas, onion, sour cream, salt, and pepper in a large bowl; gently mix together. Spoon into a lettuce-lined salad bowl and garnish with unpeeled cucumber slices. Serve immediately or refrigerate up to one hour. Makes 8 servings.

Menu

Hot Chicken Chowder
Buttered French Bread
Radishes, Carrot Sticks, Celery
Old-Fashioned Red Devil's Food Cake
Hot Coffee

This picnic features hearty hot chowder and the fixings, all carried in three vacuum bottles. The chowder is easily ladled from a wide-mouthed bottle. A square-shaped bottle, partially filled with ice, is convenient for carrying vegetable relishes.

Hot Chicken Chowder

4-pound stewing chicken, cut up
1 bay leaf
1 carrot, peeled
1 clove garlic, peeled
   Bouquet of celery leaves and parsley
1 tablespoon salt
½ teaspoon rubbed sage leaves
1 quart water
2 tablespoons chicken fat or butter
1 medium-sized onion, diced
4 medium-sized potatoes, peeled and diced
2 cups chicken stock
2 cups light cream
½ teaspoon thyme
   Salt and freshly ground pepper

Wash chicken and put in large kettle with bay leaf, carrot, garlic, celery leaves, parsley, salt, and sage. Add water, cover and simmer until tender, about 2 hours. Cool chicken in stock. Remove meat from bones and cut chicken in bite-sized pieces (makes about 3½ cups). Skim fat from broth and use 2 tablespoons of the fat to brown onion and potato. Add 2 cups of the chicken stock, cover, and cook until potatoes are just tender, not mushy. Fill a large vacuum bottle (2 quarts) with hot water to preheat. To the chowder add chicken pieces, light cream, thyme, salt, and pepper to taste. Bring to simmering point, but do not boil or the cream will curdle. Add a little water if chowder seems too thick. Makes 6 generous servings.

Old-Fashioned Red Devil's Food Cake

2 squares (1 oz. each) unsweetened chocolate
½ cup (¼ lb.) butter or margarine
1 cup sugar
1 teaspoon vanilla
2 eggs
1½ cups cake flour (sift before measuring)
¾ teaspoon soda
1 teaspoon salt
¾ cup ice water
   Chocolate frosting (recipe follows)

Melt chocolate, then cool. Meanwhile, cream the butter; add sugar and vanilla; cream until light and fluffy. Add eggs, one at a time, beating well after each addition. Blend in cooled melted chocolate. Sift flour again with soda and salt. Add flour to the creamed mixture alternately with ice water; mix well. Turn into a greased and floured 9-inch-square pan. Bake in a moderate oven (350°) for 30 to 35 minutes, or until cake pulls away from sides of pan. Cool.

Chocolate Frosting:

1 cup sugar
½ teaspoon salt
½ cup cream
1 square (1 oz.) chocolate, cut up
½ teaspoon vanilla
   Small amount of cream (optional)
½ cup chopped walnut meats (optional)

Blend together in a heavy saucepan the sugar, salt, ½ cup cream, and chocolate. Cover and boil over high heat for 3 minutes without stirring. Reduce heat, uncover, and continue cooking until frosting reaches the soft ball stage (238° on a candy thermometer). Wipe crystals from sides of pan, but do not stir. Cool. Beat frosting until creamy and a good spreading consistency. Add vanilla, and if frosting should become too thick, add a small amount of cream; beat smooth. Spread on top of cake. Sprinkle with walnut meats.

RECIPE INDEX

Photographers: Glenn M. Christiansen, pages 56, 86; Darrow M. Watt, pages 4, 8, 11, 15, 19, 20, 30, 35, 36, 44, 46, 50, 58, 61, 64, 66, 70, 72, 76, 82, 90, 91. **Illustrated by** Jane Teiko Oka. **Cover photograph by** Darrow M. Watt; menu on pages 26 and 27.